jovis

baukind — Architecture for Children
Nathalie Dziobek-Bepler

Designing Spaces for Children

A Child's Eye View

Pedagogy + Architecture + Design

— FOCUS

— PROJECTS

Strong children — for a vital society

Design at a child's eye view promotes the development of children

Architecture that meets the needs of children can be achieved when adults are willing to see from a child's perspective. By approaching children as equals, viewing the world as they do and understanding their needs, we can create environments for children that are at once flexible, stimulating, and protective. This is the unique challenge of designing any space for children, whether it be a preschool, a playground or a pediatric practice.

Children sense, think and feel differently than adults. They react to their environment intuitively and without preconceptions, and fill it with life. They engage with their surroundings by moving around, exploring and feeling. They experience a space directly, through their own bodies, and with a keen awareness of even the finest sensory influences.

This book shows how the process, from the first sketch of the building, to floor plan design and creation of individual zones, to the use of materials and color, combined with elements including acoustics, lighting and nature (water and plant design), can result in spaces that encourage communication, social interaction, movement and joy.

How, then, can we design spaces to promote children's development?

Children have different horizons and spheres of action than adults do. Baukind's projects often play with scale – employing small doors, windows near the floor, entrances to platforms that lead to cubby holes, crawl spaces or dens – elements not easily accessible to adults, but just right for children. Whether designing a climbing library, a research table or an explorable waterworld, baukind sees spaces and objects as a unity. Their aim – always and everywhere – is to foster play. And this is because children naturally learn and develop when they play. Independence, ease of communication and positive social behavior can be consequences of well-designed spaces. Wherever possible, a project's specific construction elements are made multifunctional and playful. A heating panel functions as a climbing structure, a door as a blackboard, a baseboard as a marble run. The design of these spaces should protect, inspire, move, challenge, encourage and above all support children in everything they do. If architecture, outdoor spaces, indoor rooms and furniture can be shaped to complement each other as a holistic unity, and then be rounded off with carefully designed toys and graphic elements, the result is a space where a child can truly grow.

Perhaps the biggest design challenge is managing the balancing act between complex safety regulations for spaces for children, and opportunities for exploration and self-discovery. Even required safety features can be used to offer children opportunity rather than restriction. Self-directed activity in an environment that is both open and safe allows children to discover through exploration. Children can experience making their own choices, take joy in their successes and overcome failures and obstacles. Moving about freely and making choices for oneself are formative experiences.

Children's needs can be complex and highly individual, and meeting them can require an awareness of the wide range of motor, cognitive and social skills that are still developing in a child's first years of life. It is also both crucial and helpful in each unique project to first study the particular pedagogical approaches and materials that will be used by educators and their team at the future kindergarten.

The influence of reforms in areas of pedagogy has led to more holistic approaches to learning and development. The beginnings of this kind of holistic pedagogy can be traced as far back as the eighteenth century, when the educator Johann Heinrich Pestalozzi asserted that in education "head, heart and hand" work together in concert. Today, this idea has been established with scientific certainty. It means recognizing that learning involves all of one's senses – mind, spirit and body – and that this must inform how spaces for education are designed. The goal is to achieve a balance between stimulation and rest – between feeling safe and being challenged.

This kind of design not only challenges and encourages children – it should also keep adults in mind and meet the needs of everyone involved – taking into account the space necessary for the interaction between parents and educators, for example. When a learning space is carefully designed, it supports the team in their daily work, and the broader community, too.

"We plan for children, and this should be tangible to them and to the adults."

Today, new facilities often serve multiple functions beyond their use as daycare centers. For example, in addition to the building itself and its adjacent outdoor space, we can include a daycare center's broader spatial and social environment in the planning process, and create social and community areas. This expanded social space might mean craft afternoons with seniors from the nursing home next door, sharing a kitchen with the adult education center, opening up an outdoor space to create connections within the neighborhood, or programming for joint activities with parents, youth and families – numerous opportunities for significant added value are available. If kindergartens, schools and after-school centers are closely linked to their neighborhoods and opened up to both young and old, they become meeting places, places to share experiences and ideas – anchors for the community in everyday life.

Design from a child's eye view should be considered any place where children will spend time – in public spaces, schools, doctors' offices and museums – wherever it is important to meet children as equals, to see things from their perspective and to help them find confidence in their own abilities. This confidence leads to self-directed activity and helps develop a positive self-image.

Since its founding in 2011, the architecture and design firm baukind has conceived and realized more than 100 spaces for children – projects of various sizes, purposes and construction requirements. Whether a project entails new construction, conversion or renovation, baukind's focus is always the smallest members of our society. The firm's designs translate a wide range of pedagogical philosophies into architectural concepts that support the development and independence of children through holistic design from a child's eye view.

Baukind's guiding stance is to trust the children themselves and to encourage them to act in ways that meet their own needs. The environment should be designed in a way that offers a child freedom of choice and space to move.

Holistic planning requires a team that works holistically. Thus, in addition to core architectural services, the team at baukind also specializes in designing interior spaces, furniture and even outdoor features. Baukind's design work always champions the free development of children, and this principle directly shapes the firm's corporate culture, too. All members of the team are provided the best opportunities possible to develop according to their own interests and strengths. Whether it's about children or adults: the aim should be to nourish individual potential and allow inner spaces to open.

— Nathalie Dziobek-Bepler / baukind

"It is important to meet children as equals, to see things from their perspective, and to help them find confidence in their own abilities."

01

"Well, my dream daycare center is a really huge house. The rooms change when you press a button. And it has music and a disco."

Three questions to Bobby, seven years, and Tom, six years
— the young experts

What does your dream daycare center look like?

Tom — A room with loads of huge cushions that you can use to build a really cozy den. Or a castle. And a room with a giant Lego mountain, so you can build everything you like.

Bobby — Well, my dream daycare center is a huge house. The rooms change when you press a button. And it has music, a disco and a TV, and the beds appear and disappear. Outside, the colors keep changing – you just choose the ones you want. And I like when we all splash around with water together in the bathroom. I go to school now, not to daycare anymore. In my daycare we had bathrooms for girls and boys together. In my school we have different bathrooms for boys and girls. I think that's stupid. If you have long hair like me, it's embarrassing.

What rooms do you like and when do you feel especially comfortable?

Bobby — In rooms with mattresses, so you can jump around. I also like climbing walls. And at the daycare center, my favorite place was by the window: you could lie on the windowsill, read and look out. Everyone liked the kitchen at my daycare center, because that's where we made dessert.

Tom — I feel good when I can snuggle into bed: with an audio book, a book or a film. That's so cozy! And when I have to squeeze through narrow spots and go across gorges when climbing. I like desert landscapes with cactuses, other spiky things, snakes, foxes, elephants or monkeys. With a train running through them. My favorite place at the daycare center is the play room. It has so many building blocks! Thousands of them! Long ones, thick ones, narrow ones, big ones, small ones, straight ones, slanted ones – there are so many!

What can children do better than adults?

Bobby — Children can jump, dance and run around better than adults. You are just so old that you can't run around. And even if you can, we children have magic powers! And we can simply cast a spell over you to make you a bit slower.

Tom — Definitely sports! Children can climb better because they are more agile. Yoga. And scratching our ears. And we are much better at thinking up silly things. Children can think better in general.

02 From the first places of childcare to contemporary spaces for playing and learning

Progressive teaching philosophies and how they handle space

Industrialization not only changed the world of work but also reordered or even dissolved family structures. The separation of parents and children in everyday working life started here. Children were taken care of or "kept" outside of families for the first time. An empathetic attitude towards children and their development is still a recent achievement. Starting with Friedrich Fröbel, all of the more recent pedagogical approaches describe space as an essential element in the daily work with children.

At the beginning of the 20th century, Maria Montessori (1870–1952) saw the purpose of the environment not in "shaping children but allowing them to reveal themselves."[1] For Loris Malaguzzi (1920–1994), "apart from the teacher and the other children … the school building is the 'third teacher,'"[2] an insight on which he built his concept of Reggio pedagogy in the 1960s. The pedagogic concept of Friedrich Fröbel (1782–1852) – inventor and father of the playschool – was the first to be oriented towards children's needs at the begin-ning of the 19th century. His aim was to allow children to appropriate the world through playing, because "playing is the highest form of child development."[3] Emmi Pikler (1902–1984) also took the view that children's personalities can flourish best if they can develop as independently as possible and are allowed to move about freely. Pikler pedagogy requires rooms with open spaces and simple equipment for physical exercise, so that children learn to move independently and safely.

Rudolf Steiner's (1861–1925) anthroposophical world view began in 1910 to target social justice in education, regardless of children's origins, abilities and the vocational goals of their education. His Waldorf pedagogy seeks to promote independent and free development of children, which also has implications for their surroundings. Rudolf Steiner defines very precisely what the color design of spaces should be, what materials should be used and what design vocabulary he considers to be an ideal basis for child development.

Child-friendly design is
achieved when the child's
scale is taken into account

The Danish family therapist Jesper Juul (1948–2019) places the "competent child" at the center of his view, which sees children from birth as socially and emotionally just as competent as adults. He thus concludes that children do not need education but relationships: "Children are born with all social and human characteristics. To develop these further, they need nothing but the presence of adults who behave with kindness in social relationships."[4] For Jesper Juul, the environment, just like relationships, is a flexible structure that can and should adapt and change with the children and adults who use and enliven this space.

The history of playschools and daycare centers has a grim, strict and silent beginning. It has been a long journey from a purely functional institution where children were simply kept during the day to the humanistically influenced playschool or daycare center of the present. Industrialization increased the need for childcare. Especially in England, starting in 1826 institutions were established in which up to 150 children were kept and supervised in one room. No playing was allowed; children were required to sit quietly on benches. The aim was "an early lesson in respect, order and obedience."

These grim forerunners have now been superseded and forgotten. Friedrich Wilhelm August Fröbel (1782–1852) influenced the image and concept of the playschool in the middle of the 19th century. For Fröbel, who was a pedagogue, scientist and student of Pestalozzi, children are like flowers: "You have to bend down to them if you want to identify them." Furthermore, "children … should not be merely minded and taught. Instead, they should grow, get stronger and develop happily in the sunlight."[5]

Choices that consciously break with standards and play with them direct attention to a more childlike perspective

The adjoining garden as an outdoor space at Fröbel's first playschool, founded in 1840 in Bad Blankenburg, is the central aspect of his overall educational concept. Fröbel was the first to orient this concept, along with the design of interior spaces, towards the needs of children. The children's world of experience is perceived as being of equal value and children are no longer defined as miniature versions of adults. The "free, thinking, self-acting person"[6] was Friedrich Fröbel's stated educational goal. Instead of just being supervised and monitored, the children are stimulated and taken care of by qualified educators – they learn through playing. A son of a priest, Fröbel viewed play as the highest expression of human development in childhood: children can experience the world through playing.

F. Fröbel —
"Play is the highest expression of human development in childhood."

Friedrich Fröbel brought color into educational facilities, defining "activity areas" for different pursuits and developing toys – blocks, cylinders and balls for unstructured play. The Fröbel playschool marked a decisive turning point in pedagogy that, for the first time, took children, parents, the public and the surroundings of the day into consideration. The idea of enabling self-education by encouraging play and the conviction that children appropriate their surroundings through intrinsic motivation and can learn through play are based on Friedrich Fröbel's work, which is still relevant today.

M. Montessori —

"Help me to do it myself."

A reception counter or a kitchen built at a child's scale supports children in their independence

At the beginning of the 20th century, Maria Montessori started pedagogical research into her method of orienting oneself directly towards the child, in consideration of its needs and wishes. Both a doctor and pedagogue, she argued this would allow children to become active, and that educators (adults) should take on an accompanying role. "Help me to do it myself,"[7] the core statement of the Montessori pedagogy, focuses attention on the child. Children may and should decide themselves what to occupy themselves with, what and with whom they want to learn. With this freedom, children can develop their interests and stay motivated and concentrated. This principle of freedom in education is still being pursued today as an educational concept in Montessori children's homes and schools.

In considering spaces for learning, Maria Montessori pleaded in favor of a subtle design with modest colors, arguing that children's independence should be supported by spatial design. She therefore advocated for venues with "prepared environments" that would train the senses and provide stimuli for learning. In Montessori pedagogy, ordering elements are an important aspect of how a space is designed. To offer orientation, rooms should be clearly structured and straightforward. "It is not the child who should adapt to the environment, but we who should adapt the environment to the child,"[8] she proclaimed.

For the design, this means a change of perspective: it is not enough to ergonomically adapt furniture to a child's scale and place materials within children's reach; only spatial clarity gives children the full freedom to play and make decisions without their attention being unnecessarily distracted. They are thus able to realize their own wishes and interests more easily. And communication within a group of children can also be facilitated.

The experience of self-efficacy and a self-confident and creative attitude towards the environment necessarily also lead to a creative way of dealing with problems and overcoming them independently. Maria Montessori was able to show that the more independently children can act, the more self-confident and socially competent they become.

M. Montessori —

"It is not the child who should adapt to the environment, but we who should adapt the environment to the child."

A coat rack without hooks allows children to act independently

Although the Montessori method has boomed especially in Germany since the PISA study in 2001, Montessori facilities were still a rarity in the 1960s and 1970s. In the Italian province of Reggio Emilio, Loris Malaguzzi developed his Reggio pedagogy approach during this period. Similar to Maria Montessori, Reggio pedagogy also views the child as the creator of its development, knowledge and ability. Children know best what they need and develop their own competences. The spatial surroundings become part of the educational concept in Reggio pedagogy. Children should perceive the daycare center as their home territory and actively shape it. They derive their potential not only from their individual interests and abilities but also from active interaction with their environment.

L. Malaguzzi —
"Space is the third teacher."

Malaguzzi sees spaces as a "third teacher." In Reggio pedagogy, the spatial surroundings offer children a sense of belonging, while at the same time stimulating them to take on new challenges. Such spaces are furthermore characterized by openness and transparency, allowing them to support communication and cooperation and to stimulate children and allow scope for development. Accordingly, children playfully discover their spatial environment as part of their world.

Loris Malaguzzi categorizes the clear but flexible functional designation of spaces into three types: the piazza as a meeting place and central "village square," in reference to Italian village life; the atelier for trying out and experimenting; and the activity zone of the dining area, which is usually directly connected to the piazza with an open kitchen.

Children should be able to develop freely and in a self-determined way

The notion of children as the protagonists of their own development and environment led in the 1970s to the educational concept of open work. Group rooms were opened up and replaced by activity-specific, functional rooms: a creative room, music room, experimentation room, exercise room and a room for role plays instead of traditional group rooms. Children can decide themselves where they want to be and are motivated to try out various areas and follow their own interests. Children must consider the following questions: where do I want to spend my time today? Which kids do I want to play with? Children learn to assume social responsibility and to take care of themselves. The educators are merely companions and observers of what is happening. The children themselves choose a key caregiver by deciding who they feel comfortable with. The concept of open work is also widely practiced in schools today.

As children's development and education opportunities are always strongly determined by a child's family background, work that considers social environment is increasingly gaining in importance in playschools. This includes comprehensive considerations of the whole system surrounding the child. Parents are integrated as partners into everyday playschool life, so that the educational process can be shaped together. Other family members and residents of the district are also invited to participate. Daycare centers are increasingly gearing their services also to these groups and offer family education, parental/social/legal consulting, self-help groups, parent cafés and neighborhood parties.

Opening a social space means including other institutions and their programming in the work of the daycare center. Cooperation with care facilities for the elderly represent true added value for both children and senior citizens, thus helping to strengthen society and broaden people's horizons of experience.

The German pedagogue Friedrich Fröbel, the Italian primary school teacher and pedagogue Loris Malaguzzi, the Austrian-Hungarian pediatrician Emmi Pikler, the Italian doctor, progressive educationalist and philosopher Maria Montessori, the Austrian publicist and esoteric Rudolf Steiner, and the Danish teacher, social pedagogue, family therapist and author Jesper Juul: as significant pioneers, all of these figures decisively influenced and reformed the history of pedagogy and its relationship to architecture and space. Their standpoints and motifs may differ in some points, but they nevertheless have many aspects in common.

Pedagogues at playschools and schools make use of these ideas today, reconfiguring them to create their own educational concept. Spatial environments can and should support these educational concepts.

*Learning from each other
and laughing together*

03 "Without a doubt, spaces are a third educator for children, they are part of the team."

Markus Schindler has been an educator at the Spreesprotten daycare center in Kreuzberg for nine years. Since 2018, he has been pursuing his vocational training as a family therapist at the German-Danish Institute for Family Therapy and Consulting. He works in the interiors of a playschool designed by baukind.

Montessori, Waldorf, Fröbel or Reggio: there are many different educational concepts. Which do you find particularly convincing? — In my experience, no concept can be dogmatically enforced. For a start, given that each group is always different and has varying requirements, as an educator one must always remain flexible and keep asking oneself every time: "Why is it so important to me to have this rule? Is it to protect myself, is it arbitrary or just a convenience?" There are good educational approaches that have brought about rethinking or even a revolution in their time. I see it more like a puzzle. You have to find the matching parts: tailored to yourself, but primarily to the group of children.

What are the principles that guide your work at Spreesprotten? — The focus for us is on the relationship with the child, in accordance with the approach of Jesper Juul and his conflict management, because his ideas are very flexible, incredibly honest and simple. We view ourselves as a life companion for the children. Therefore, we do not position ourselves above the children. We are there and share the space with them.

Jesper Juul's educational approaches are not a traditional pedagogical concept, though. — That's right, for us the focus is simply on the relationship with the child. For children, adults are a reflection of feelings, because they have the words for them. Children always want to cooperate. You can't enforce rules and cooperate at the same time. For Jesper Juul, it is about not making decisions on behalf of a child as an adult. To what extent am I prepared to reflect on myself? This is the basis of work with children and with people in general: to always

question oneself. For me, this has nothing to do with age, it is a basic stance. Everyone can learn this; it's never too late.

Does that mean that you yourself would refer to your profession differently? — I find the notion of educator very derogatory. We have by now gained a different picture of childhood: each child has its own individual personality from the beginning and our work is about supporting children on their own path. I see myself as a companion for this stage in life and want to be a good example for children, showing them how to live within a society. I see the daycare center as an additional element of the family, not as a family replacement. I like the idea of a color palette: it is not about replacing red or green, we are simply adding yellow and blue.

What are your experiences and observations when it comes to child-appropriate spaces? — Children always look for their niche. An environment is appropriate for children if it is designed from their point of view. However, the point is not at all to provide as many options for play as possible but to offer a stimulating environment. The spaces can be very sensitive to personal needs, and not only to those of the children. If a space like the cloakroom is designed in a very open way, it makes it easier for me to work with the parents: I can keep an overview, listening with one ear to the children and at the same time communicating with the parents. I am currently experiencing this myself because of the change of the children's group. I now work in rooms that are well thought out and designed, which makes everyday work a lot easier. Even the floor drain in the bathroom allows me to approach the daily bathroom routine with a new sense of ease.

Markus Schindler is an educator who is training as a family therapist

The spatial surroundings become a third educator?
— Absolutely, the spatial environment is a third educator for the children. The rooms are part of the team. Interiors need an appealing atmosphere, a clear structure and childlike, playful details, such as a special heating cover or color design. However, design also starts very subtly. A good example of this is acoustics. As an adult, I can say when it is too loud for me. Children are usually not yet able to do so. Through suitable acoustic conditions, rooms become significantly more pleasant for both children and adults. A design of space that is sensitive to these needs should be holistic and consider all aspects of the space – not only the ones that are visible.

How can pedagogy and architecture mutually support each other – go hand in hand in developing new directions? — We educators have a check-in week once a year and then consider together: what did the children play with and what did they leave alone? What about the spaces is important to us? Since a groups fills the space with life in a way that is always changing, it is important for spaces to have a flexible design. Architecture can create a smart basic framework that divides areas cleverly. Filling the space is then the task of the educators, together with the children. A space is never finished; it rather functions like an organism.

And what have you yourself learned from children?
— An incredible amount (considers). Reflecting emotions was an important experience for me because I did not experience that in my childhood.

> **"A space is never finished; it rather functions like an organism."**

Are girls and boys different?
— Yes (laughs), of course they are. The question remains, however, as to how much of that comes from the way they conform to norms they find in the world. There are quite a few children who do not fit into clichéd notions and would like to behave differently. My wish would be for children to grow up free from these expectations and to orient themselves towards their needs and feelings, their own character.

Why do we also need child-friendly design outside of the playschool, school and similar places?
— I would like to be able to move around with children in the city without worrying. In Sweden, for example, there is a pedestrian path network that is completely separate from vehicle traffic. Many dangers cannot be avoided even by being careful and considerate. A lorry driver simply cannot see the child standing next to his wheels. At the same time, the most important asset for children is their independence. As a child, I grew up in a village, could walk to school alone, and we took it for granted: the streets were ours! We definitely need more child-friendly design for public space.

04 Movement — the driver of development

Design that inspires movement

Movement is a basic need for children and their first and most important form of communication. Movement enhances wellbeing and a feeling of self-worth. When children experience that they are capable of achieving something, that their actions have a consequence, their positive self-image is strengthened.

It is elementary for children to feel and try out their physicality, to experience successes and failures directly on and with their own body. These experiences have an effect far beyond the development of motor skills, which are closely connected to cognitive development.

Neuroscience findings show that physical activity and using all of one's senses lead to the formation of synapses and the activation of neurons. Especially early childhood experiences of movement have a significant effect on the brain and memory.

Nowadays, children spend a lot of time indoors and don't move enough. Obesity and a lack of exercise are the consequences. "While for adults, two to three physical exercise sessions of about 60 minutes a week can be considered sufficient to maintain physical capacity, children need daily exertion of at least two hours to develop their organic functions,"[9] states Dieter Breithecke, a sports and kinesiology scientist.

There is a saying: "Falling over is part of learning to walk." When designing exercise facilities, designers must consider the wide spectrum of age and developmental differences and the necessary safety measures. It is a balancing act between safety and what children can or should be assumed to be capable of. The aim is to create spaces that do not slow children down but encourage them to discover their environment by moving freely.

— Where and how can movement be encouraged?

Fluid floor plan

Open spatial concepts with connections between the rooms allow space for movement. A central arrangement and the use of corridors as play areas allow children to move freely at their own pace. Circuits through several rooms, from inside to outside and back again, encourage children to move.

Stairs

Stairs offer a whole range of movement options. They are a meeting place, a playing object and their function in itself makes them an activating element. If slides, caves or climbing frames are added to them, the result is a diverse spectrum of movement.

Platforms

Built-in elements and elevated platforms extend the space and offer storage space for mattresses, sports equipment and toys. Especially in smaller facilities where space is a real luxury, such solutions are of great value and allow additional room for movement.

Loose elements

Balls and cushions extend the physical experience. Children can act out their urge to move in all directions in a ball pit. Loose pads are both building material and gym equipment and offer children a free, creative and self-determined form of movement.

Ramps and steps

Steps, slopes, ramps and slides are playing magnets and stimulate movement across all ages. It does not take much to turn a little platform into a motor challenge and open up new worlds for playing and movement.

First experiences of movement

Seemingly small details can present a real hurdle for toddlers. Even small differences in height, bars to hold onto and freely swinging elements represent a test of courage and are a training ground for physical development.

The corridor can
become a racing track

Even the bathroom
can be an invitation
to move about with
complete freedom

Fluid floor plan
— off to the races

Race courses and play alleys can be included and taken into consideration from the outset when designing the floor plan. Children love getting faster or running in a circle. The aim of a good spatial design should be to provide a place for these natural needs and preferences. Designing rooms as dead ends should be avoided wherever possible: connecting doors instead allow for an uninterrupted flow of movement and exuberant running in circles. A piazza is well suited to running around, and even in a bathroom you can play tag around a central washbasin.

Group rooms with doors to the garden form an indoor-outdoor course to run around. To keep dirt outside, large doormat areas should be planned at each door.

Long corridors are perfect for races and can also be used for riding children's vehicles. Attention should be paid to skirting boards being high enough so that walls dont get dirty or damaged. To avoid the risk of injury, door handles should curve inwards.

Moving in circles — thinking about how children will move through the space should be part of the floor plan layout

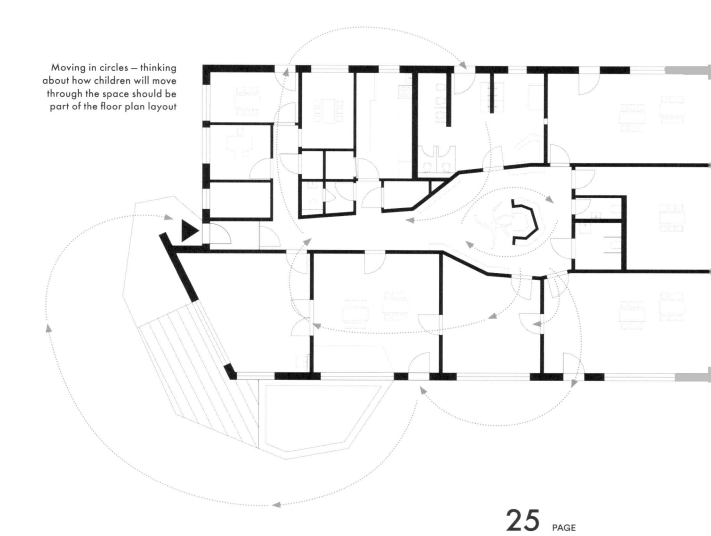

Stairs — multitalents that inspire movement

Stairs inspire movement. It is always worth incorporating stairwells as spaces for movement and playing. This requires close coordination with fire protection planners right from the planning phase.

While cautious voices insist that stairs should be avoided in daycare centers because they harbor danger, others say that they train the coordination of movement and promote motor development.

Including intermediate landings can reduce the potential length of a fall. Apart from railings for adults, there should always be railings for children. Slides can be ideally combined with stairs. Stairs with wave-shaped steps are easy even for toddlers to climb. If stairs are fitted with soft materials such as carpet or linoleum, they become a popular meeting place, a podium or a reading corner.

Adding 15 m² of space
and fun on two extra levels

Platforms
— climbing tower
and crawling den

Play podiums, raised levels and climbing elements provide variety for movement and physical challenges. They extend the available space, complement spatial zoning and open up new perspectives.

Climbing, crawling, jumping – built-in elements stimulate all sequences of movement and physical senses. An elevated play level promotes undisturbed activities in small groups and can be anything that children's imagination can make of it: a boat, a space station, a castle in the air. Accident insurance companies stipulate the height from which coverage for falls is required.

Ramps and steps — make them move

Ramps, slopes and slides are exciting for children of any age. Even a small difference in height encourages children to move.

Young children crawl up ramps and steps, while older children use them as a race course with vehicles. Steps provide additional levels and help children to adopt other standpoints and perspectives.

A ramp inspires children and is a place to practice motor skills

Ramps help children pick up speed
and can be incorporated into any game

Loose elements — creative chaos

Ball pits and loose pads create space for free movement and creative chaos. All children enjoy immersing themselves in a ball pit. It trains their perception, sense of balance and proprioception. They can practice dexterity skills such as grasping, throwing, aiming, catching and collecting in a playful way. For older children, the pit should have a depth of at least 30 centimeters, for toddlers, on the other hand, only 15 centimeters.

Loose pads on platforms and benches are cushions for parents and teachers, while for children they are large building blocks for free play: carrying, lifting, stacking. Gross and fine motor skills are trained, while spatial awareness is raised.

Mobile pads form the boundary
for a flexible ball pit

Platforms at different heights or small bumps
in the floor create impulses for movement and
train children's sense of balance

First experiences
of movement
— stimuli for toddlers

Movement in early childhood is not the same as
movement of older children. Depending on their
age, children's capabilities vary greatly, and so do
the stimuli they need to foster development. For
toddlers, slight level differences between platforms or a small bump in the floor are already a
big challenge to be mastered.

Crawling landscapes – consisting of mats, bars
to hold on to and ramps specially geared to the
requirements of toddlers – support the development of gross and fine motor skills.

Toddlers initially tackle height differences of five
to ten centimeters and they can fall safely on
cushions. It is valuable to practice falling over and
this boosts self-confidence. It is not about going
higher, further, faster – it is often small details that
encourage children optimally.

Bars and mirrors
encourage the little
ones to stand up

Ramps with attached
strips are easier to climb
by small children

Small differences in height
are deliberate trip hazards

05 Multifunctionality —more is more

The door is a blackboard, the baseboard is a marble run, the platform with matresses is a climbing frame

Children's imagination knows no boundaries. If the surroundings are flexible and multifunctional, their imagination can flourish freely. Places, buildings, rooms, furnishing and objects must therefore be adaptable. Alterable furniture and rooms that offer more than one function and long-term potential always remain exciting – especially for children who in their early years are developing physically and mentally day by day. In a daycare center, multifunctional elements and flexible structures are of elementary significance and practical relevance, because multifunctionality and ambiguities allow the use of a space to be maximized.

A table is more than a surface for eating and drawing. A table can be anything. For a toddler, its size alone can make it a house: the infant sees four supports and a roof. If you turn it on its side, the table is a protecting wall. If you turn it upside down, it might transform into a ship, a car or a whole castle. Some adults have lost sight of this magic.

The tool for this is called imagination. Children have fewer inhibitions. Their limited knowledge and comparatively few experiences form the basis of their creativity and fantasy. Children question and explore their surroundings, automatically becoming inventive.

Design cannot and should not simulate this fantasy world of children but should give it room to flourish. The more abstract the starting situation, the more possibilities for interpretation it allows: a heating cover becomes a musical instrument, banisters are a perfect slide, a niche becomes a hiding place.

— Where and how is multiple use possible?

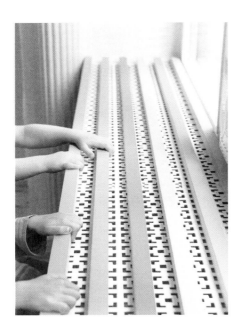

Storage space

Storage space and playing possibilities can be ideally combined. Especially for smaller facilities, this represents a valuable space gain. If shelving, a platform with mattresses and a sideboard are optimally designed, they invite children to play, romp and climb.

Radiator covers

The necessary protective radiator cover becomes a play object: climbing frame, reading platform, musical instrument or marble run. Creative approaches bring together several functions in just one element.

Walls

Walls provide great potential. Whether as a creative and display surface or for providing information – a clear design offers a framework for different uses and ensures a calm and uniform overall appearance.

Functional furniture

Multifunctional furniture supports the multiple use of a room and facilitates everyday routines at the daycare center. An exercise room can therefore quickly become a painting atelier or an exhibition space, or the room can be divided into zones.

Play furniture

Play furniture is an all-rounder: stools become a bus. Straight ahead, then right, next stop: lunch. And after lunch, the table becomes a shop. A modular furnishing system allows constantly changing play worlds and makes quick and space-saving stowage easier.

Pads and mats

Seat cushions and sleeping mats are ideal building materials. They are soft, flexible and lightweight, serving as perfect building blocks for huts, castles and other fantasy worlds, as well as providing comfortable seating.

Radiator covers
— safety combined with play

In daycare centers, radiators that are hot or have sharp edges must be covered for safety reasons. These covers should also have the potential for play, if possible. Children can climb, balance or read on them. The necessary protective cover becomes a place for children to play or spend time.

There are no limits to design possibilities here. Radiator covers can become a musical instrument or a marble run, a weaving frame or any other sensory element. Attention must be paid to always ensuring the necessary air circulation. The radiator must also be accessible for maintenance purposes.

The bars on the radiator become a favorite place to play in the winter — warm and with a view

Marbles roll from the radiator cover, across the baseboard and through the whole room

The children call this radiator cover "crocodile"

Secret entrances to caves and
hiding places on the shelf

Storage space — play space

A lot of materials accumulate on the premises of children's facilities. Some, such as mattresses for the midday rest or gym equipment, are used daily but usually only briefly. They are bulky and take up storage space.

A storage space that children can play in is a huge space gain, especially for small facilities. Platforms extend the usable area of a daycare center. At the same time, they serve as exercise equipment, stages or hiding places. Even tidying up and storing can become a game, encouraging children to take on responsibility.

Mattresses disappear in the steps

Cleaning up becomes part of the play and promotes independence

A fluorescent map of stars turns
the corridor into a planetarium

Blackboard paint on the facade offers
space for art — until it rains again

A weaving frame in the
wall paneling — creative
design with found objects

Linoleum on the wall repels dirt
and is also a creative tool

Walls
— usable boundaries

Walls provide large areas that can be designed
and used. A wall becomes an atelier, a gallery or
a place to communicate information. It becomes
a work of art if partial areas can be painted on
and animated. When covered with linoleum,
a wall serves as a durable and dirt-repellent
painting base and is at the same time an optimal
display surface.

Using magnetic or whiteboard markers, the
wall itself can present information; additional
pinboards or information panels are no longer
necessary. Delineating the area helps to keep
an orderly, clear and calm appearance, despite
wide creative freedom.

"Lost and Found" — to collect
leftover clothing

Transparent whiteboard paint turns any
wall into a communication surface

Functional furniture — versatile utility

Cupboards and shelves usually take up a lot of space. If they are mobile, they allow many additional uses: they become room dividers, atelier walls or display surfaces. Open shelves encourage autonomy: children can independently take out the toys or art materials they like.

If shelving is fitted with castors, the back can become a large painting atelier. Here, children can paint on large-format sheets standing up. In daycare centers without an atelier room, this extends the educational space. The rear side of the reversible shelving is also suitable as a gallery and display area.

Flexibility and multifunctionality of the furniture facilitate the daycare center's day-to-day routines, which means more space and makes it possible to integrate several functional areas into one room.

The backs of the mobile cupboards serve as a canvas, a table turned over is a shelf for brushes

Play furniture can be
anything — a climbing course,
a store or doll's bed

Play furniture
— no need for toys

Multifunctional children's furniture is both a
practical furnishing and a toy. Stools that can
be turned over have a different sitting height
depending on which side is up or down and
are therefore suitable for all age groups.
Stacked together, they form a highchair.
Tables and stools can be practically stored
by being pushed under each other.

For children's furniture to be suitable for playing, it should be lightweight and there should
be enough grip holes for easy handling. Children
use the stools like large building blocks. Pushed
together, they become a dolls' bed or bus, while
tables turned on their side become tunnel and
cave systems or a shop.

For parents it's a comfortable place to sit,
for children it's lightweight building blocks

Pads and mats
— brilliant blocks

Whether as seating platform, foam shapes or mattresses – pads are versatile playthings. They serve as sleeping mats in a quiet room, as seat cushions in cloakroom areas or as seating cubes for the staff. If cushioned elements are not fixed to their base, they turn into big, soft building blocks, rolling wheels and house walls. If the colors are coordinated with the walls and other surfaces, the result is a harmonious overall appearance.

06 Waterplay — immersive sensory experiences

Water is a fascinating element and offers hands-on lessons in physics

In the bathroom, children experience with their own body and all their senses that water is warm, cold, squirts unpredictably or flows slowly; that it falls downwards, collects and runs off, can be channeled and absorbed with sponges. Water is versatile. We drink it and swim in it. We smell and taste it, feel its temperature, hear it dripping and splashing, see it flow, feel its force or gentleness in a water jet.

While the focus at a swimming pool, splashing pool or water playground is clearly on relaxation and sensory experiences, bathrooms – which are primarily intended for daily body hygiene – can also be designed with an additional focus on wet fun and play. For children, the bathroom landscape then becomes a popular learning and play area. Instead of just washing their hands or brushing their teeth, children enjoy spending time in the bathroom most of all because of the water itself. They want to splash, to experience, to feel.

In Germany, building regulations and size standards for bathrooms in daycare centers vary according to the federal state. In Berlin, 0.6 square meters of floor space per child must be planned for the bathroom. Therefore, the bathroom in a facility with 100 children must have a minimum size of 60 square meters: ample leeway for a creative and innovative design!

Children play, experience and explore water for hours in children's bathrooms. Educational water games support perception and sharpen the senses. At the same time, the bathroom also promotes social learning. If there are fewer taps and washbasins than children, the group must coordinate and agree. The bathroom becomes a negotiation space. If dams and water channels are built together as a group, the game becomes a communal project.

Elongated washbasins with different levels and damming devices let the water flow and be channeled: waterways inspire the imagination. A varied choice of different tap fittings teaches the respective mechanical use by turning, tilting or pressing. Shower areas are designed for free splashing, so that the whole body can get wet in this zone and playing can be wild and free.

—How do children's bathrooms become a world of experience?

Construction standards

By using acoustic ceilings, underfloor heating, pleasant lighting and natural materials, the quality of bathrooms as a place to spend time is greatly increased. If the interior standards are carefully planned and realized, children will spend hours playing with water.

Water troughs

Playing with water together becomes a varied experience if stepped, elongated or freestanding washbasins are used. Water channels with different fittings, levels and damming devices are ideal for playing as a group.

Creative tiling

Tiles in the bathroom serve the purpose of hygiene and are quick to clean, but they also afford a wide range of design possibilities. Whether glazed tiles, mosaic tiles, porcelain stoneware or colorful grout – the look and atmosphere of the bathroom change fundamentally if tiles are used skillfully.

Wall color

As the time spent in a bathroom is limited, one should have the courage to use color, which can be striking in sanitary rooms. If the tile and wall colors complement each other, the overall impression is harmonious.

Openings and portholes

Interior windows and openings from the bathroom to the hallway or adjoining group room create a visual and acoustic connection and encourage communication. The resulting visual axes make supervision easier for the staff.

Blackboard walls

Blackboard walls or dark tiles serve as a drawing base and are optimally placed in bathrooms. Large-format chalk pictures can be quickly washed away with a shower-head without leaving any residue.

This Kneipp pool
fosters health and fun

Construction standards — how a bathroom becomes a wellness landscape

Children love playing with water and can spend hours in bathrooms. To make the time spent there as pleasant as possible, it is recommended to consider the fit-out standards. Acoustic ceilings should also be installed in bathrooms, because it gets loud when a lot of children are playing at the same time! Underfloor heating allows children to play with water for longer without getting cold. The additional installation of a tube radiator can be helpful for drying wet clothes.

Atmospheric lighting is very advantageous – natural daylight is desirable but is not essential. Wooden accents have a warm effect and create a pleasant playing atmosphere.

Floor tiles should have antislip properties, so that playing with water does not harbor the risk of injury. A floor drain helps to remove flooding. Rubber flooring can also be used in children's bathrooms, as it is warm underfoot and easy to clean.

The water runs through all the basins

Water troughs
— let the water flow!

Playing with water fascinates children and fosters social development. Working together on dams and reservoirs requires good communication.

At elongated washbasins with different levels and damming devices, children channel the water, build reservoirs and play together. Different basin heights and depths are important and a must, so that children of all ages can reach taps and basins.

The use of different tap fittings trains different sequences of movement – turning, pressing, tilting. The different handling of the taps and the regulation of water pressure extend motor experience when playing with water.

The basins themselves should be made of easy-care materials such as ceramics, tiles or mineral composites. The latter is very soft and its use therefore reduces the risk of injury in case of a fall. Scalding protection should be installed at every washbasin.

The water temperature is thus permanently restricted to around 40 degrees and the risk of injury is reduced. Plastic baskets are suitable for storing water toys. The baskets should be perforated so that toys dry quickly.

Playing together with
water is social learning

Creative tiling
— artistic highlights

The choice of colorful floor and wall tiles is almost unlimited. Tiles primarily serve the purposes of hygiene and easy cleaning, but they can also become a decorative gem. They fulfill their function as splash guards behind washbasins and WCs and should be used more sparingly on the other walls, so that the atmosphere in the bathroom is not too cool. Floor tiles must have antislip properties and can also be an enriching design element.

If a tiled picture is designed together with the children and staff, the bathroom becomes a participatory space.

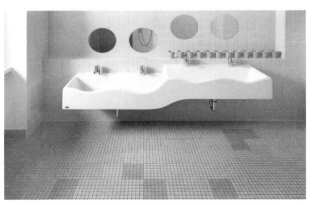

The high joint count in mosaic tile prevents slipping

Rounded shapes can also be created with tiles

Mosaic tiles can be used
to make rounded edges

Wall color — simple means, great effect

The color design in the bathroom can be significantly more vibrant and bold, as children usually spend less time in washrooms than in group rooms. The colors of tiles and walls can be in similar or contrasting shades to create a harmonious overall appearance. Painted murals can be realized more cost-effectively than pictures in tile.

If one wishes to change the design in the future to give the bathroom a new character, this can be realized quickly and easily by painting the walls. Walls in the bathroom should be painted with Latex paint, as it is abrasion-resistant, durable and impermeable to water.

Neutral tiles are timeless in terms of design, and repainting the walls gives the bathroom a new look every time

Color on the wall continues the tile
pattern and completes the overall design

Openings and portholes — peekaboo!

Interior windows are an unexpected and interesting element in the bathroom. Openings at child height encourage communication throughout the interior, providing visual axes and spatial connections. They allow staff a quick glance into the bathroom to make sure everything is in order, while giving children the feeling of not being alone. Openings near ground level enable shortcuts into the bathroom – only for the children.

Peepholes connect rooms
and arouse curiosity

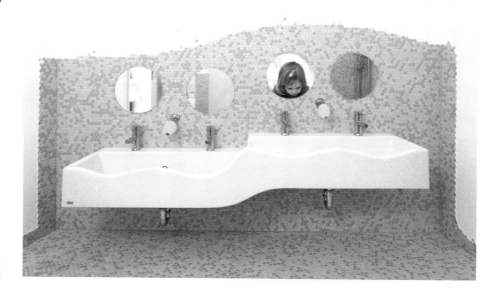

Surprise!
You are my reflection

Blackboard walls
— the bathroom becomes
an artist's studio

A shower is mandatory if children under the age of three attend the daycare center. The shower area is the perfect place for a blackboard wall and can be integrated into the wall design by using blackboard paint. Dark, unglazed tiles are also suitable as a drawing base. The chalk dust is simply washed away with the shower – which makes cleaning easier for the staff and is also fun for the children.

If blackboard walls are incorporated in the shower area, attention must be paid to good sealing to avoid water damage. Dark tiles in the shower area provide both protection against water and a surface for creative drawing.

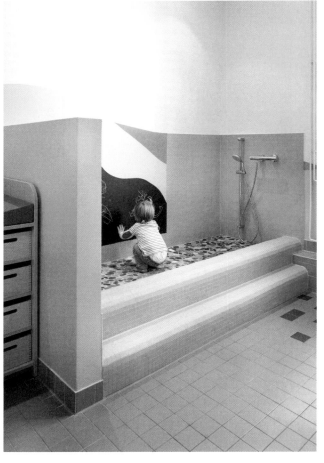

Shower areas are ideal places for blackboard walls — paint and then just shower it all away

07 Transitional spaces — the quality of the in-between

From a neglected threshold space to a lively place for playing and encounters

A room is a firmly defined area, usually with a designated use. But what about the areas that connect these rooms, that come either before or after them? They are usually not taken account of in the design, even though they harbor great potential.

Hallways, cloakrooms, entrance areas – transitional spaces connect, divide and filter, they are places for meeting and interacting. Transitional spaces welcome us and bid us farewell. A corridor can – like a street – by all means be a place for spending time: especially if it widens into a hall, like a square.

In educational care facilities, transitional spaces should also be considered and conceived as an active component – not least because they usually take up a relatively large amount of space. If the corridor is upgraded through architectural means, it can function as an additional dayroom for the whole daycare center, becoming a place to play and an educationally valuable space.

In the cloakroom, some children experience feelings of insecurity and the pain of separation. The cloakroom is a transitional space – from the familiar surroundings of one's parental home to that of the daycare center. Caregivers and toys are not exclusively available but must be shared. This is a hurdle for children that needs to be overcome daily – which is sometimes easier and sometimes more difficult. Well-designed entrance areas and cloakrooms can facilitate this transition.

As entrances, corridors and cloakrooms have a function that is not primarily education but mainly distributional, yet it usually only requires a few cleverly employed choices to turn the transitional space into a play area.

This results in free space for spontaneous meetings, movement, a sense of belonging and social interaction, along with feelings of safety, retreat, relaxation, peace and quiet. Children can experience the underestimated quality of the in-between.

—How does the in-between become a hive of activity?

Changing room

Cloakrooms are places of arrival and departure. If their design is inviting, it makes the transition easier for the children. Outside of drop-off and pick-up times, they can be used as an additional play area.

Piazza

With a piazza, the entrance area of a daycare center becomes the focal point and centerpiece of the facility. Rooms are functionally connected and transitions have an open plan design, creating a space for community and communication.

Play corridor

Play corridors represent additional educational space. If rules for fire protection allow it, playing platforms and exercise elements can be integrated and a valuable play area is created.

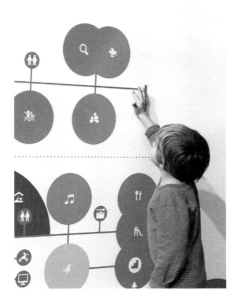

Gallery walls

Corridors are an ideal gallery space. Here, children can actively participate in decorating the daycare center, as the corridor provides a space for their works to be admired. Exhibiting the children's works of art, photos and discoveries invites parents to take part in the everyday life of the daycare center and their children.

Guidance systems

Good and quick orientation eases the children's transition to everyday life at the daycare center. Guidance and orientation systems can be integrated into the wall design. They must be intuitively comprehensible. Often the clever use of color is enough.

The cloakroom should be
integrated into the design concept,
as the welcome mat for visitors

Changing room
— hello and
good-bye

The cloakroom plays a key role at an educational facility: this is where the children arrive, where they are welcomed and part with their parents, which is for children often a painful process. Over the course of the day, the traditional cloakroom is an unused area and therefore lost space. However, with the right design, it can become a high-quality space for spending time.

If the cloakroom is spacious, there is a feelgood atmosphere at drop-off and pick-up times, and the children can also use this space during the day for playing and as a retreat. Seating and playing platforms can simultaneously serve as storage space for wellington boots or outdoor toys.

A well-designed cloakroom also takes the parents into consideration, providing them with seating. Furthermore, important conversations between parents and staff often take place here. If adults enjoy being in this area, their mood will positively influence the children.

These seating platforms
offer storage space for
rubber boots

Platforms are not just for climbing and sitting
— they are also practical places to get children dressed

Good acoustics and natural light
provide a pleasant atmosphere

Piazza — a vibrant gathering place

The idea of a piazza as a valuable part of a daycare center goes back to Reggio pedagogy. The entrance area is not conceived as a corridor but more as a central market square and meeting place. The piazza creates an open and flowing spatial connection, offering enough space for movement and free play. Existing daycare centers often do not have the space for a piazza, but a corridor can also be transformed into one. Accent lighting and a seating platform can turn the corridor into a meeting place.

A piazza can also serve as a changing room

Play corridors
— valuable added space

Corridors connect rooms and are usually not paid much attention beyond this function, even though they offer plenty of space for playing and can enrich everyday life at the daycare center. If corridors are considered in the planning as spaces for playing and movement, this must be done in close consultation with fire protection planners. These officials check whether the installation of playing and seating platforms is permitted. Such elements turn the corridor into a stage, reading corner or obstacle course. Loose elements such as pads and seat cushions complete the playing options, generate coziness and are stowed away at the end of the day. In order for corridors to work as day rooms, good acoustics, a suitable temperature and atmospheric lighting are required.

A play corridor allows children to develop social contacts beyond the boundaries of their own group

Sound installations, sensory elements and platforms transform the corridor into a space full of experiences

Loose pads serve as building materials and and also provide comfortable corners to read

Gallery walls
— an invitation to be creative

Corridor walls are ideally suited to exhibiting the children's works of art, photos, discoveries and souvenirs. Whether it is themed pictures, gathered autumn leaves or photos of the last group outing – children have the possibility to actively contribute to the decoration of their daycare center, with space for their works to be admired. In the gallery, parents gain a glimpse into the everyday life of their children and the whole group.

Wooden boards or stretched-out rubber bands serve as a base and for affixing items. Ideally, these systems allow the children to put up and take down their works independently. The use of push pins should be avoided for safety reasons. A structure designed on the wall with a clear outline creates an organized athmosphere the overall appearance of the corridor.

The varying children's artworks
give new looks to spaces

Large gallery surfaces invite children
to take on the decoration themselves

The animal buddies show the
way to each of their rooms

Guidance systems
— orientation for everyone

Guidance systems show children and adults the way through the daycare center. Good orientation fosters a sense of security and supports the children's independence.

Rooms and directions can be found more easily and identification with the facility and group are visually supported. A clear and intuitively comprehensible visual language makes guidance easier to follow. The guidance system is adapted graphically to the design of the interior spaces, creating a harmonious overall appearance.

Children use magnets to mark the room where they want to spend time

08 "Clear spatial structures help children's imagination flourish freely."

Karin Schmidt-Ruhland, professor at the art college Burg Giebichenstein University of Art and Design Halle, has been directing the study course and master's program in design of playing and learning since 2007.

How do you, as an expert in design of playing and learning, define the concept of child-appropriate design?
— If the design is oriented towards the capabilities and requirements of children. This is not just about ergonomic aspects. Playing products, for example, should allow room for creativity, be intuitively usable and offer children the possibility of free interpretation: less is more. In general, people are the focus in the design of playing and learning, and we include all generations. This design is concerned with lifelong playing and learning. However, it is especially children who need opportunities to play, whether with objects, products or in their surrounding space.

How do you identify a good learning toy?
— As I see it, a toy is something other than a learning tool. Playing is defined as an activity that is carried out for enjoyment only. For this you also need objects and spaces, for example for role playing. In the process, children relate to the world and of course learn something, too.

So when playing, you are supposed to learn automatically. Isn't that contradictory?
— No. The question is whether the focus is on learning or playing. It is the purpose that makes the difference. Every occupation leads to an extension of skills and abilities and that's why children also learn naturally when playing.

Lego, Playmobile or wooden toys: what makes a good toy?
— If a toy prescribes too much – functions, switches, building instructions – children will play with it once, and then it will just sit on the shelf. This is why Lego bricks are great. A child can freely interpret the toy, use it differently and play with it in a variety of ways.

And it isn't left on a shelf ...
— No, of course not! Because it offers endless number of possibilities for interpretation.

Do you have another example of a good toy?
— Let's stay with building blocks. If I have many elements of something, even many of the same elements, then I can do a lot with them. Allowing for variety and leaving interpretations open: that is what characterizes a good toy product. To give an example: for children, a stick can also be a horse or a cooking spoon for their doll.

What role do product design and design play, if a simple stick can, for children, be a horse?
— A significant role, I think – and in aesthetic education, too. The variety and open interpretation I just mentioned are important. And toy products are also often a miniature version of products for adults. Again, the key is role playing, imitating and one's own interpretation. When designing, we have to make sure that we take children seriously and make objects available to them that are authentic, and that they can also animate with their own imagination. As a designer, I have to look closely and not cater to any preconceptions.

How do toy designers work? What do your students learn?
— I teach them that the focus is on people and that people need to be considered. I have to observe people without prejudice and draw conclusions from what I see. In order to train this observation sequence and to establish a relationship with the children who will later use the products, we have a playschool at the college in Halle and thus a research and trial site.

Karin Schmidt-Ruhland is a designer and professor for the design of playing and learning

You have your own laboratory. Do you also pursue a particular educational concept at the playschool?
— Our concept of cooperation is oriented towards shared participation. The educational concept of Burg-Kita is characterized by a variety of approaches from Montessori to Reggio – put into practice by the staff and the children. Cooperating with us, children are also our testers for new models and products we develop. We observe them intensively and gain new insights from how they act.

What influence does good design for interior spaces have, in your experience? What makes a space child-appropriate?
— If the space meets the child where they are and the child has the possibility to try things out for themselves in the space. This kind of design is about free space. Freedom to play only develops if there are physical spaces that are not limited by short-lived and pre-defined things. Clear structures and a basic spatial order help children's imagination flourish more freely without steering it in a particular direction. Children use most objects multifunctionally and are exceptionally creative. Here, too, the rule applies: less is more.

What needs do children have today? Were they different in the past?
— I think that basic needs always stay the same. The children of today experience different influences, which lead to the development of new needs. We do not yet know what consequences it will have if you spend the whole day just moving your finger on a smartphone. Simply going outdoors on your own, as I was still able to do in my childhood, which allowed me to conquer my world, is rare today.

And children's rooms?
— They look different nowadays. Children's rooms are packed!

"Allowing for variety and leaving interpretation open."

Do children today have too many toys?
— Far too many! The design of toy products is often overdone. On the shelves of toy shops, you can find countless superfluous and unsatisfactory products, but people buy them anyway. In order to change that, one would have to start with the adults. Whether I am in Nuremberg at the toy exhibition or in Milan at the furniture exhibition: we people always want something new. But perhaps the children of today, with their crammed playrooms, will do it differently later when they are parents themselves.

Why is it important that adults do not forget to keep playing?
— We adults do not forget how to play, but how to play freely. Which means proceeding without a plan, doing something for enjoyment alone, to clear our heads. Apart from that, we all play like mad. We love games, soccer for example. I find that just as we should learn throughout our lives, we should also play casually for our whole lives.

The needs of everyone involved

Various spaces accompany people in all stages of life, including its beginnings. A sensitive design of interior spaces, balanced between stimulation and a sense of safety, fosters childhood development and supports children in their independence and self-development. The challenge is to reconcile the needs of the children, educational team and parents on the one hand with legal directives and safety regulations on the other, and to meet these requirements in the design.

Children need spaces where they feel at ease and an environment that stimulates them in order to foster their personal development. Retreat and stimulation complement each other to form an overall structure that is openly organized and well structured, offering all children spatial orientation and an overview. Children's basic need for safety, protection and care must be fulfilled to enable children to explore their surroundings without fear and to experience a feeling of freedom.

Architecture can make a significant contribution here. People constantly interact with their environment. Children are also, even especially, sensitive to the atmosphere of the rooms where they spend time. If children are received in surroundings that convey a sense of security while also offering stimuli, then this environment can be considered child-appropriate. A variety of surfaces, materials and structures train the sensory perceptions of children. Platforms of different heights and climbing possibilities allow a change of perspective. Meeting points support interaction, and modular furniture fosters self-determined creativity.

Apart from children's needs, healthy and good working conditions for the educational staff must be considered in the planning: retreats for breaks, documentation and administrative work; ergonomic requirements for the furniture; and visual axes that ensure a good overview. Special meeting rooms with a quiet atmosphere allow a focused discussion with parents, beyond cloakroom chitchat, and can also be used for workshops and information events. Use beyond everyday childcare routines is aimed for in new facilities and is a prerequisite for many new builds. The principle of dual use can apply to the rooms for discussions, therapeutic work and

Rules and regulations

group events, as well as the kitchen. This multiple use saves resources and links the facility with its surroundings and other institutions. Parent and family education services can and should be integrated. Networking with youth centers, retirement homes and the immediate neighborhood is actively encouraged, thus opening up the social sphere.

How does a daycare center come to life? 09

Architecture and its possibilities

Just like other construction tasks, architectural ideas and designs must comply with legal directives, safety regulations and technical specifications. For a daycare center building, these are relatively complex. The planning must observe all the directives regarding acoustics and sound insulation, barrier-free access, lighting and ventilation. It must comply with fire protection, hygiene and indoor climate regulations. In practice, this means, for example, ensuring minimum illuminance and sufficient emergency escape routes, laying nonslip floor coverings, avoiding stumbling hazards and other injury risks. Almost every country has its own complex regulations, laws and guidelines in this respect.

There are countless models worldwide for tending children, which differ according to children's age groups and the times of day when they are being cared for. Facilities for this purpose may be called daycare centers, playschools, nurseries and the like. Nurseries, for instance, basically take care of children ranging from infants to an age of three years old, while three- to seven-year-olds go to playschool.

Daycare centers are organized either as state-run or independent facilities, which are funded in various ways, for instance by parents or by syndicates. They all have the purpose of providing childcare for working parents.

The construction task of a daycare center is a balancing act: it must fulfill requirements and legal regulations as well as planning law. Light and color, material and acoustics, accessibility and scale – all of these aspects must be taken into account if spaces are to provide children with both safety and a challenge. Often it is precisely these challenges that harbor great opportunities for fostering child-hood development.

The overarching question is how design can work within this framework and open up possibilities. When architecture, the design of the interior spaces, and furnishings harmonize with the basic educational concept, spaces are created that allow children to grow.

What must each room in a daycare center provide?

The floor plan of a daycare center should always be developed in conjunction with the educational concept of the facility. Knowledge of the requirements for the individual rooms and areas, together with dialogue and cooperation between the users, educational staff and planners, allow a balance to be achieved between design and budget, vision and reality.

A children's restaurant — In a children's restaurant, meals are enjoyed communally. If there is a children's buffet with open compartments at a child-appropriate height, children can take their plates and silverware independently and set the table themselves. A durable floor covering such as linoleum and good room acoustics are recommended. If the furniture is flexible and stackable, the room can become an exercise room or atelier outside of mealtimes.

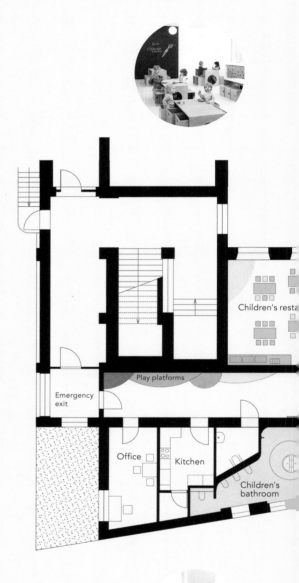

Play corridor — A well-designed play corridor invites children to run around and play. It allows children to meet and establish social contacts beyond their own groups. The corridor can serve as a presentation space for the children's works of art or become an atelier in itself. If fire protection allows, playing and reading platforms can be integrated. Acoustic ceilings should be installed in every play corridor.

Office and staff room — The office is used to take care of administrative tasks and as a room for parent meetings. Staff rooms are places for the pedagogical staff to retreat and have a break. Their design should be pleasant and inviting. It is desirable to provide two separate rooms for office work and breaks, although in small daycare centers the necessary space for this is often not available.

Children's bathroom — The children's bathroom is a place for personal hygiene and should also provide the possibility to play with water. Bathroom fittings and washbasins should be planned at a height suitable for children. A generous changing table with steps facilitates work for the staff. A children's bathroom can invite children to play and move, becoming an important educational space. A washbasin with varying heights, walls usable as blackboards and a splashing area are valuable measures. Nonslip floors are mandatory, while an acoustic ceiling is recommended.

Group and themed rooms — Depending on the pedagogical concept, children are tended in group or themed rooms, such as the atelier, craft room or research room. Children need activity and relaxation zones in the form of niches, platforms or dens, as well as the opportunity to meet as a larger group. They should be allowed to use the rooms flexibly and to participate in creating them. Optimal room acoustics and lighting are important.

Relaxation room — A separate room should be provided for midday naps and relaxation periods. If the mattresses are stored in platforms, then the room can also be used for playing outside of the rest times. Soft floor coverings such as carpet and good room acoustics are just as important as the possibility to create different lighting atmospheres.

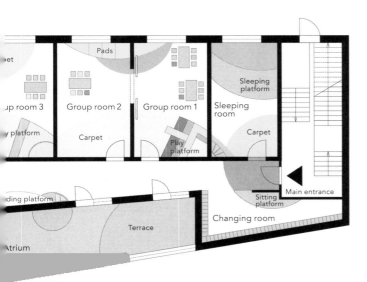

Entrance — The entrance area should be friendly, inviting, barrier-free and as spacious as possible. Here one should find information about current matters and forthcoming events. Seating for parents should be provided. The entrance door must allow escape in the event of fire and be secured so that children cannot leave the premises unnoticed during operating hours. A large doormat area helps to keep the daycare center clean.

Changing room — The cloakroom is a transitional zone to daycare center life. This is where parents bid farewell and staff and parents chat in passing. A sitting area provides a pleasant setting for these conversations. Each child is assigned a cloakroom space with a coat hook, shelf and shoe compartment. These should be set up so that children can use them all by themselves. A cloakroom is ideal if it can be used as a play area outside of changing times.

Planning requirements

Fire protection

Children are particularly in need of help in the event of danger – e.g., a fire. It must be possible for the personnel to save the children as quickly as possible at all times, as the children may not be able or allowed to leave the building on their own in the event of fire. Fire protection plans must be drawn up for every daycare center and approved by experts. Attention should be paid to short escape routes and that emergency exits are kept free at all times and can be opened from the inside. This requires complex door systems, because it must be simultaneously ensured that children cannot leave the premises unsupervised.

Lighting

Daylight is considered the most pleasant kind of lighting, with a positive effect on the health and wellbeing of people. All rooms in a daycare center should therefore have a high incidence of daylight. Natural daylight allows the children a wider range of sensory perceptions than artificial light, for example, through changes in the quality of light over the course of the day.

As daylight alone is not enough to illuminate rooms all year round, additional artificial lighting is necessary. The dimensioning of the lighting system depends on the use of the rooms and the associated visual tasks.

Apart from the necessary minimum illuminance, the color of the light is also crucial: warm white light with a color temperature of under 3300 Kelvin is perceived as cozy and pleasant. All the light fixtures used should be ball-proof, glare-free and mounted out of the reach of children. The installation of several switching circuits allows partial darkening and lightening of specific areas of the room, so that different atmospheres can be generated. Direct and indirect lighting should be available.

Acoustics

Many daycare centers are louder than a major building site. Noise levels of 80 dB(A) and higher are easily reached. Many studies have proven the negative effects of noise on staff and children. It is therefore essential to ensure good sound protection and good indoor acoustics in daycare centers.

Noise insulation refers to measures that reduce the transmission of noise from a noise source to the recipients. Suitable measures (for example elastic surfaces, heavy components, separation of components, sound-proof windows, acoustic ceilings), can reduce the transmission of noise from the outside into the daycare center and vice versa.

Measures ensuring good room acoustics are important to absorb the noise in a room, enabling good speech intelligibility and optimal audibility. Reverberation time is one of the most important criteria for evaluating room acoustics. The installation of highly absorbent acoustic ceilings has been proven effective for regulating reverberation time. In addition, room acoustics can be improved by means of wall absorbers.

Indoor climate

A healthy indoor climate helps to safeguard health. In addition, a pleasant indoor climate is conducive to wellbeing and quality of life. The target value for common rooms in daycare centers is 20°C. In rooms where children get changed or wash, up to 24°C should be the target value. In all rooms facing outwards, windows ensure natural ventilation. For rooms facing inwards, such as cloakrooms or sanitary areas, mechanical ventilation should be installed. A temperature of 20°C is also recommended in corridors and stairwells, as these are often also used as play or educational areas.

 ## Hygiene

At a daycare center, there are many hygiene-relevant areas, including the bathrooms, kitchen, children's restaurant, clothes compartments in the cloakroom areas, playing corners and niches. Observance of hygiene guidelines goes without saying at daycare centers. The overarching purpose is the health of the children and educational staff. Interior materials used in daycare centers must be free from harmful chemical substances. In addition, materials must be cleanable with water, disinfectant-proof and robust. Water services should be operated at temperatures that prevent Legionella growth.

To prevent the transmission of diseases, minimum distances between items of clothing or towels must be guaranteed in the cloakroom and sanitary areas.

 ## Accident prevention

The building, the interior fittings and the outdoor areas are to be designed to minimize the risk of accidents.

In addition, there are organizational and educational measures that reduce the risk of accidents. On the one hand, it is therefore important to educate children to behave in a safety-conscious manner, but on the other hand, it is also essential to train their motor skills, as accidents are often caused by a lack in motor coordination.

Special precautions must be taken when designing furniture or building elements. Potential trapping and abrasion hazards must be avoided.

 ## Accessibility

Daycare centers are publicly accessible buildings and should therefore be planned and built barrier-free.

Particular consideration is given to the needs of people with physical restrictions (e.g., with mobility aids or wheelchairs), or with eyesight or hearing impairment. It may also be necessary for the daycare center to have a barrier-free bathroom. Wide corridors, sliding doors and transitions without thresholds, ramps instead of stairs and contrasting guidance systems ensure safety. In multistory daycare centers, it is necessary to install an elevator. Wheelchair access should also be part of the planning. In the outdoor area, the paths should be wide and even, while floor surfaces should be suitable for wheelchairs and have a contrasting design.

10 "There should always be room for chaos."

Nathalie Dziobek-Bepler worked as an architect in New York for five years and subsequently at Graft Architekten in Berlin. Today she runs her own architecture firm in Berlin. Her team has realized a wide range of projects with a focus on child-appropriate design for interior spaces. These projects are always centered on children. In 2021, baukind celebrated its tenth anniversary.

What can and should we adults learn from children?
— The way that they are unbiased. How they are playful, nonreflective, uncontrolled, impulsive. We usually lose all of these abilities as we get older. Watching children disappear into their own worlds, without caring what those around them think, is what I find most awesome. I love that in children.

Do you incorporate this way of thinking into the planning of your projects?
— Always. Children should be presented with rooms that they can participate in creating – quite contrary to the basic presumption of many adults that a room must look perfect. I think there must always be room for chaos to develop, despite an ordered structure, which is also necessary. We as designers determine this structure, which is the basis for chaos to spread (laughs). These spaces should be rooms in which children create their own worlds. Just as a childs bedroom should – as far as possible – be created by children themselves.

You adapt your designs to the respective pedagogical concept of the clients, although "open work" as an educational concept appeals to you in particular. What is special about it?
— If you, like us, trust that children have the competence to take care of themselves and act according to their needs, then this basic attitude enables open work. Instead of traditional group rooms there are an atelier, craft room, lab room or a room for role play. Our aim is to design the surroundings with appealing possibilities in such a way that the child can move around and

choose as freely as possible. Family therapist Jesper Juul said: "Do not draw the boundary around the child, but around yourself." If we are aware of our boundaries, we can grant children more freedom.

If money, time and structural engineering were negligible, what would your dream daycare center look like and why?
— It would be totally flexible. The rooms could constantly be rethought and arranged differently – by children and adults. The kitchen would be designed so that children can participate in cooking every day, at their worktop level. It should be in the center of the facility and have a very open layout – similarly to how the fireplace was at the center of family life in the past. There would also be large and wild outdoor areas with animals, which would be also allowed into the daycare center. Life with animals is an incredibly valuable experience for children. And in my dream daycare center there would be just as many male as female staff! A retirement home and daycare center would be housed in the same building – with shared meals and activities. Luckily, this already exists, but is still much too rare and not implemented consistently enough. Of course, rooms for such communities present particular challenges. I would really enjoy working on this.

What are the challenges for you as architects and designers when planning interiors and buildings for children?
— The task of building a daycare center is a complex special area with many obstacles and an incredible number of regulations. In the meantime, we have become very familiar with

Nathalie Dziobek-Bepler is an architect, mother of three and the founder of baukind

"Because spaces influence and shape people, they also have the power to change society."

the requirements of youth welfare, building authorities, health authorities, food authorities and accident insurers, which are unfortunately often contradictory. We advocate for all these regulations and requirements to be brought together in a guideline for daycare center construction – but unfortunately, this doesn't exist yet. It would help all those involved to raise building for children to a different level of quality.

Has design for children changed?
— In the ten years we have been involved in this field, there have been changes in the way children are viewed and also in pedagogy. Open work as a pedagogical concept is significantly increasing, and possibilities for exercise and movement are being accorded greater importance within everyday life at the daycare center. We try to facilitate movement in spaces such as the cloakroom, corridors and even the bathroom.

Is it necessary to convince the clients of your concepts?
— We begin by intensively engaging with the pedagogical concept of the client. Whether

we are dealing with a forest playschool or Montessori approaches to church playschools, there is a wide range of orientations that we must of course be aware of. Some clients simply want a normal building application for a renovation. Just the way they have always done it and the way it has always been. We need a good understanding of our clients in order to see where there is leeway in preconceived ideas. Is it possible to develop something new together? As we all know, tastes are different. And we are a team player and work together with our clients to find the best solution for the respective project.

Why this book?
— Architecture and design are enormously important because of the effect they have on people. Design can change lives. Spaces influence and shape us. How do children grow up, how do people develop – and how can architecture support this development? And because spaces can influence and shape people, they also have the power to change society. I have a deep inner drive to participate in shaping and enriching society. Our interiors and buildings seek to bring people together.

11

From urban structures to untamed nature

Fröbel Daycare Center
775 m² for 65 children
Berlin / 2019

Into the wild — a jungle for city children. The daycare center in the newly developed Mediaspree district combines modern clarity, ordered chaos and untamed nature.

Pedagogy — Relationships, individualization and participation are the three basic pillars supporting the educational work of FRÖBEL Bildung und Erziehung gGmbH. Out of the conviction that children are curious by nature and want to explore the world with all their senses, the playschool in Berlin-Friedrichshain follows a concept of open pedagogy. The children and their needs are at the center. The basic condition for open work is that the children explore all the rooms independently and are supervised according to their development.

Architecture — The daycare center for 65 children is situated on the office campus at Mediaspree, which was completed in 2019. The facility is on the ground floor of a futuristic-looking office building, with direct access to the outdoor play area, and was created as a playschool close to the headquarters of a large tech company.

The office building was built according to the gold certification standard of the Germany Sustainable Building Council (DGNB). For the daycare center, too, materials were chosen that have a high health and environmental compatibility in terms of their production, processing, function and disposal.

Concept — The design is based on the idea that children need order and structures, together with wildness and freedom, to develop and flourish. Accordingly, the interior design represents a progression from the city and its organized urbanity to untamed nature: natural green and earthy shades, authentic materials such as wood and exposed concrete, and tangible nature in the middle of the city. Analogous to the three pillars of the pedagogical stance of the client – relationships, individualization and participation – the design is also divided into three zones.

In the group rooms, the parallel lines dissolve and become diagonals, joined by green — as a color and in the plants serving as a transition to the garden.

Lines continuing from the interior to the exterior give the outdoor space a sense of life and create a connection with nature. This area offers a wealth of experience for the senses, places to climb, and natural retreats.

The children's restaurant is connected to the kitchen by a large glass wall. Outside of eating times, the space is used to play.

In the entryway and corridor, the colors are restrained, the forms are clear and the lines run parallel — a reference to the city.

In Zone 1, the children are welcomed into a structure that still has an urban appearance. It forms the transition from the city and their home to the daycare center. In Zone 2, one finds the day rooms, where the strict structures gradually dissolve into diagonal lines, complemented by bolder colors and built-in units with an open design. Plants become part of the interior and serve as a transition to the garden, which forms Zone 3, with an abundance of nature and playing possibilities.

"Play is never trivial; it is serious and deeply significant."

— F. Fröbel

The bathroom is a play landscape with a washing trough for playing together with water.

The pedagogical concept of open work at the Fröbel Daycare Center is supported by clear zones and open built-in units. The themed rooms, which address different needs and offer space for activities such as climbing, building, and experimenting, as well as for reading or resting, enable both shared and individual activities. The open character of the rooms is reinforced by the window area, which stretches across the whole facade facing the interior courtyard. Indoors and outdoors merge, sunlight enters the rooms and nature becomes part of the playschool. Different perennial plants allow nature to be enjoyed in winter, too, forming natural retreats and islands.

The playschool in Berlin-Friedrichshain brings together the city and an experience of nature. Ordered structures, nature that has been tamed and wild freedom merge into each other. The design of the inside spaces provides what children need in their environment to grow up happily: safety and freedom.

Zone 1

The path from the city into the daycare center. The lines still run parallel, and the colors grey, white and brown dominate the spaces.

Urban structure

In the entrance area and in the corridors, the urbanity of the city extends into the playschool. Straight lines and grey color shades dominate this area. Components and furniture are linear, with exposed concrete and screed floors mirroring the urban space. The lights on the ceiling are also arranged linearly and at right angles.

In the cloakroom, the waiting area for the parents and the corridors, individually placed plants hint at the green interior world. The color green shows the way to the main rooms. Materials such as wood and rubber ensure a natural appearance and an inviting atmosphere.

The platforms in the entrance area play with the rectangular language of urban forms

A cuddle cave with a window on the inside looking into the group room

Plants give a hint of the green island inside the daycare center

Zone 2

In the themed rooms, the static lines are broken up, leading the children into a world of green and earth tones — nature has come inside!

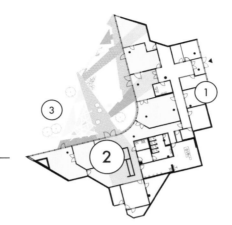

Tamed nature

In the themed rooms, the ordered structures are broken up. Nature and greenery cut their way into the daycare center. The platforms made of oiled wood and the rubber flooring vary in brown and green shades.

Oblique lines, wild trees and lush indoor plants represent a tamed wilderness. Ramps, swings, a slide and ball pit invite children to climb and play.

The open plan rooms enable flexible use, and the wide range of playing options can be used by the children according to their individual needs. The big glass facade allows an open view into the garden – the wilderness is right nearby!

The children themselves take turns in caring for the plants

Oblique lines create
dynamic spaces

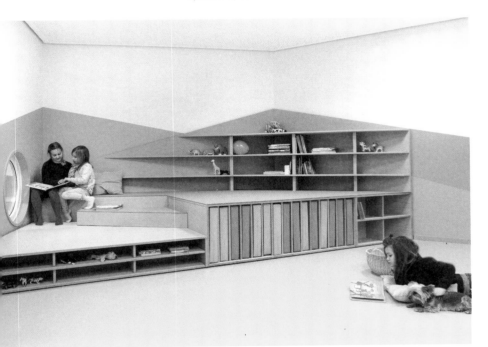

Zone 3

The lines running from the interior to the exterior define different play areas — a living structure for natural chaos.

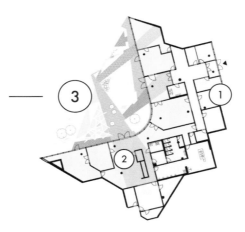

Creative wilderness

A network of dynamic lines continues from the interior to the exterior, where wild and free nature clearly dominates.

The garden is divided into areas for different places and motor skills: activity areas, retreats, grass landscapes and a barefoot trail. It is designed for children to experience nature — by touching, smelling, tasting. In the urban gardening area, the children plant raised beds and pots together. Perennial plants enliven the outdoor area all year round. They are design elements and become part of how the children play.

Urban gardening allows children to actively shape their environment

Elevations and a barefoot path make the ground into something to be felt and explored

Prairie grass brings the wilderness right into the city

The children experiment and play together on the seven-meter washing trough with cascades, dams and various tap fittings

"It has become impossible to get the children out of the bathroom."

— Preschool teacher / Fröbel Daycare Center

The bathroom is a play landscape with a central washbasin for playing with water together. Different tap fittings extend the physical experience with different heights, water pressure, angles and handling.

Apart from playing with water, the walls are also playthings and can be used for large-scale chalk drawings. The staff are also happy about this practical aspect, as the walls can be cleaned easily with a showerhead. In the seven-meter-long water landscape, the children can experiment together and gather valuable experiences: How do I dam water?

How does it flow? A game that is otherwise only possible for children outdoors, in streams, is brought inside and simulated thanks to many basins, steps and damming options. The children's bathroom therefore also adheres to the motto "Into the Wild" – making it possible to experience nature even in the city.

Dark, unglazed tiles make for
an ideal painting surface

The washing trough's different heights allow water play for children of all ages

— 01

— 02

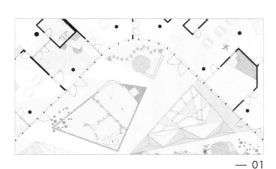

— 03

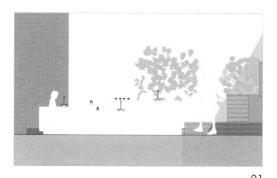

From first sketches to the daycare center

— 01

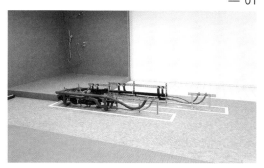

— 02

— 03

— 01

— 02

— 04

12

My color, my group

Weltenbummler Daycare Center
765 m² for 85 children
Berlin / 2019

From color island to color island — corners in a single color create zones in the open plan rooms, aid orientation and define groups.

Pedagogy — The Berlin Institute for Early Childhood Education and Complementary Childcare (bik. e.V.) pursues a holistic approach. Family-oriented services are integrated to supplement the childcare. Discussion and therapy rooms are accommodated in the building. The concept of the daycare center pursues a development-centric and childoriented approach in homogeneous age groups. The educational focus is on encouraging self-determination and initiative among the children: letting them discover, allowing them to try out and do things themselves – accompanied by regular learning activities offered by the staff.

Architecture — The planning task not only consisted in designing a children's daycare center but also in defining a design guideline for other facilities – a corporate architecture. As a pilot project, the Weltenbummler Daycare Center is intended to be a model for all bik e.V. facilities to be planned in the future.

The design elements therefore had to be flexible and transferable to other premises. A color code was developed that is reflected in the interior fittings, in outdoor play elements and in the wall design.

Open rooms with a clear color scheme help the children easily find their way around the building

Concept — The educational work of the Welten-bummler Daycare Center, with a strong focus on the children's independence and division into homogeneous age groups, was translated into a color-based design concept. The subtle color scheme of the basic elements is contrasted with monochrome color accents in more striking shades. This structures the open plan rooms and facilitates orientation for the children. In the communal rooms, such as the bathrooms and cloakrooms, and in the outdoor area, all the colors come together to form a harmonious overall appearance.

The play tower uses different heights between the terrace and the outdoor play area and fosters rich play for children of all ages.

EG

The common room is used for therapeutic activities, workshops, conversations and celebrations.

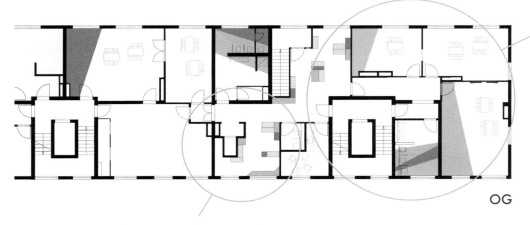

OG

Because several age groups share a cloakroom, its colors are mixed. There is ample space that invites one to spend time, with comfortable seating islands.

"For us, it has always been about more than just being a place for children to play and meet. The children should learn with and through their surroundings."

— Mirjam Spitalsky / managing director bik e.V.

The colors mix in the outdoor area, because this is where the children's groups and mixed-age groups spend their time. Still, there are areas that offer places for retreat and rest, along with age-appropriate incentives for movement, especially for the younger children.

Strong, monochrome color corners mark the group rooms and make orientation easier — each color, with its room, is for children of one age group.

The layout of the Weltenbummler Daycare Center is reminiscent of a map. The color islands serve the purpose of assigning children to an age group and help the children with spatial orientation. The children feel a sense of belonging, according to the motto: my color, my group.

In the communal rooms such as the bathrooms and cloakrooms, as well as in the outdoor area, all the colors are mixed and show the children: these spaces are meant for all of us.

The association bik e.V. is involved on many levels with the field of early childhood education and complementary childcare, research, consulting and further education. Accordingly, its facilities always include rooms where seminars and other events can be held for parents and staff. These rooms are not outsourced but an integral part of the layout concept. The daycare center is therefore open to many themes and people. It offers families comprehensive support and advises them on matters that are relevant beyond the daycare center itself.

At the Weltenbummler Daycare Center, 80 children are tended in homogeneous age groups. Each group is assigned to a certain age and development stage. This means that over the course of their time at the daycare center, the children pass through all the group rooms.

On the ground floor, the area for those aged one and a half to four, warm and vibrant colors in the yellow-red-orange spectrum were used. The group rooms for the four to seven-year-olds are on the upper floor, where cooler colors in the blue-green spectrum form a contrast to the colors used one story below.

The basic colors of both floors are beige shades that form a gentle background to the vibrant accent colors. Linoleum was used as floor covering throughout the daycare center.

Each color island offers suitable age-appropriate activities. The scale of the elements, such as steps, obstacles and ramps, is adapted to the respective age group. The children find important age-appropriate challenges that they can learn from and grow with. Every year, the children and their group move into a new group room, where they can discover new caves, niches, corners and freely hanging bamboo canes that they can use for dangling and swinging.

All the podiums provide storage space for toys, learning utensils and mattresses for sleeping or resting on after midday. The podiums are made of multiplex panels, oiled in color and in some areas covered with carpet.

In the bathrooms and changing rooms, the colors of the individual groups mix

In the entrance area, the stairs with a colorful wooden railing welcome children and adults – in everyday daycare life this becomes an educationally valuable space. Older children like to sit and spend time here, while toddlers love to keep climbing the stairs.

One side of the slats is colored, reflecting the colors of the overall concept. The slats allow views from and into the stairwell while also protecting against falls.

To be able to use stairwells educationally, fire protection planners must be consulted. It is always worth doing this, as it means being able to create additional play area and storage space on and under the stairs.

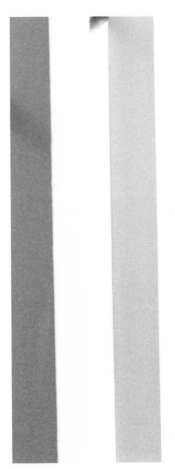

Small differences in
height become an exercise
course for toddlers

Playhouses encourage
movement and promote
communication

The idea of the indoor spaces is continued in the
outdoor area, which all age groups share use of.
Echoing the indoor design, the colors red, yellow
and purple define the areas for the younger
children outdoors, too.

The terrace, stairs and garden provide motor
challenges for children of all ages. The terrace
with colorful climbing balls is covered with rubber
granulate, providing the necessary protection in
case of falls.

All the play equipment is made of squared timber.
The gaps between the timbers afford interesting
views. Depending on the perspective and location,
the elements appear transparent or closed.

"In the garden there is a huge climbing house. There are a lot of spiders, which is a bit yucky."

— Marlowe / four years old

The rope course and the play tower with a slide are used by the older children. The play tower links the terrace and the sandpit playfully, with its design principle corresponding to that of the houses for the younger children. To ensure safety here as well, there are more difficult climbs in the form of 40-centimeter-high steps. This precents children under three years old from getting into areas that are not safe for them.

This detail also shows that at the Weltenbummler Daycare Center every age group is considered and taken care of individually – always with the goal of bringing everyone together as a community.

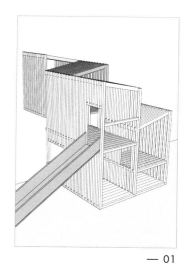

— 01

— 02

From first sketches to the daycare center

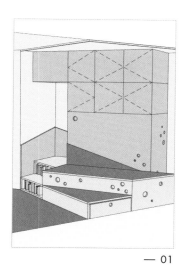

— 01

— 02

— 03

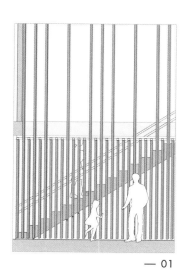

— 01

— 02

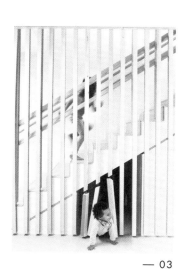

— 03

13

Sailor's yarn, harbor air and foghorns

CompanyKids Hafencity Daycare Center
750 m² for 80 children
Hamburg / 2016

Nautical worlds of experience at the CompanyKids Daycare Center at the heart of the Hamburg HafenCity.

Pedagogy — The provider PME Familienservice works according to a holistic concept. The educational work ranges from the promotion of physical activities, as advocated by Pikler and Hengstenberg, to natural science education, put into practice on the premises as a semiopen concept. Organized into daycare groups, the children are encouraged to move independently through the building and the themed rooms. The childcare offer is supplemented by a range of services supporting the compatibility of family and work.

Architecture — The headquarters of PME Familienservice in the Hamburg HafenCity were completed in 2016 and house the offices and an in-house academy, alongside the company playschool. The brick building typical of the HafenCity and designed by APB Architekten was realized within a construction period of two years. All the ground-floor rooms facing the street have a ceiling height of around five meters. The design challenge lay in making this height something that could be directly experienced and sensed.

Concept — The location of the daycare center and the offices at the heart of the Hamburg HafenCity determined the theme: waterways and port scenery shaped the design concept, which comprises the daycare center, the adjoining office and seminar rooms and the academy. This results in a uniform

design for all the functional areas of PME Familien-service. Fenders, buoys, floes, shipping containers, a lighthouse, ropes and other maritime elements are implemented in the form of carpentry components together with platforms, cloakrooms and stacks of mattresses – always abstract enough not to limit children's imagination. The aim of the concept was to make open work accessible to experience in exciting themed rooms and to design the two-story building with the help of a color scheme so that the children can easily find their way around.

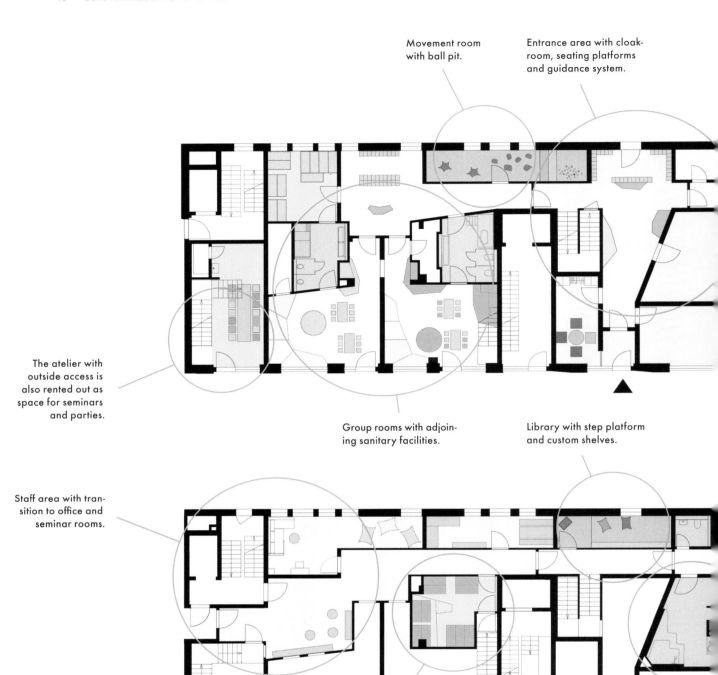

Movement room with ball pit.

Entrance area with cloakroom, seating platforms and guidance system.

The atelier with outside access is also rented out as space for seminars and parties.

Group rooms with adjoining sanitary facilities.

Library with step platform and custom shelves.

Staff area with transition to office and seminar rooms.

Relaxation room where up to fifteen children can sleep.

Water world with splashing area and cascading washing trough.

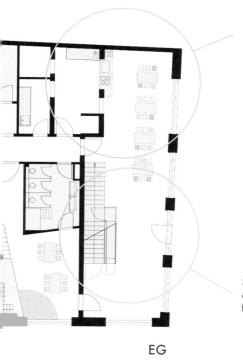

Children's restaurant, sports room and event room with an open kitchen.

Stairs with slide and a climbing frame with storage.

EG

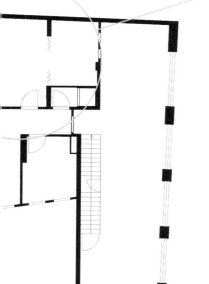

Workshop room for learning and role play.

OG

"For us, the focus is on the children. Our aim is to convey knowledge with joy and without pressure."

— Margit Werner / PME Familienservice

At the CompanyKids Daycare Center, 80 children are tended in three groups. The group rooms for the two baby and toddler groups for children aged from eight weeks to three years are on the ground floor. Each group has its own sleeping room on the upper floor, accessed via internal stairs. The group of older children has a group room on the ground floor and otherwise uses the themed rooms spread over both floors.

The themed rooms comprise a bathroom landscape, a library, a craft room, a learning workshop, a role play room and an atelier. The multifunctional children's restaurant that is used as a sports room outside of mealtimes is a meeting place for all the children.

On the first floor there is a transition to the office and seminar rooms of PME Familienservice. This ensures that the services can be optimally networked.

According to the concept of open work, children can decide themselves in which of the various themed rooms of the daycare center to spend time: the craft room, research room, library or bathroom landscape.

So that children can be quickly found in the large two-story daycare center by staff, and by the parents who come to pick them up, an oversize guidance system was placed in the entrance area. The layouts of both floors are shown in abstract form on this magnetic wall picture, which was developed by the designers from urbn pockets together with baukind. Each room is indicated by a simple symbol. Using this interactive wall picture, the children communicate what area they are currently in.

The cloakroom area and the whole entrance area are designed with the theme of a harbor landscape. The lights on cables that were left visible are reminiscent of harbor lanterns, the boxes for personal belongings in the cloakroom are little shipping containers, and the room divider resembles a picket fence from the port area surrounding the daycare center.

Seating podiums in the shape of floes are an invitation to take a seat and allow parents and educators to talk to each other. The entrance area with a friendly and inviting design offers plenty of space and provides a relaxed drop-off and pick-up zone for parents and children.

The guidance system in the entrance area makes it easy to find your way

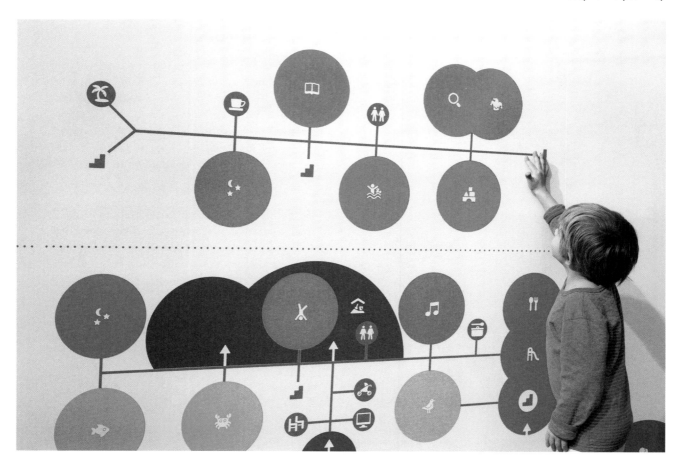

Small height differences in the play mats,
grab bars and mirrors define a stimulating
landscape for toddlers

Clippings near the
floor create connections
to the outside world

"I like things to climb on, all kinds of stuff for building and rainbows."

— Edith / four years old

In the group rooms for toddlers there are wall motifs made of wood relating to the design themes, which stimulate the children to move in a number of ways: bars for pulling themselves up and learning to stand, mirrors, and soft mats for their first attempts at climbing to cushion any falls. Even a few centimeters of height difference challenge toddlers motorically and support physical development. A window sticker, which takes up the design vocabulary, shields the rooms on the ground floor from the view of curious passers-by. Openings near the floor, however, allow the children to look out.

The CompanyKids daycare center pursues the movement concepts developed by Pikler and Hengstenberg. All the rooms include movement elements, alternating with relaxation zones. The children should enjoy discovering their surroundings independently and be able to try things out themselves.

For the older children, there is something very special: a multistory climbing unit that stretches up to the ceiling, making use of the full height of the room. The high platform provides extra space and can be used for playing and as a retreat.

The multilevel climbing unit uses the entire height of the room

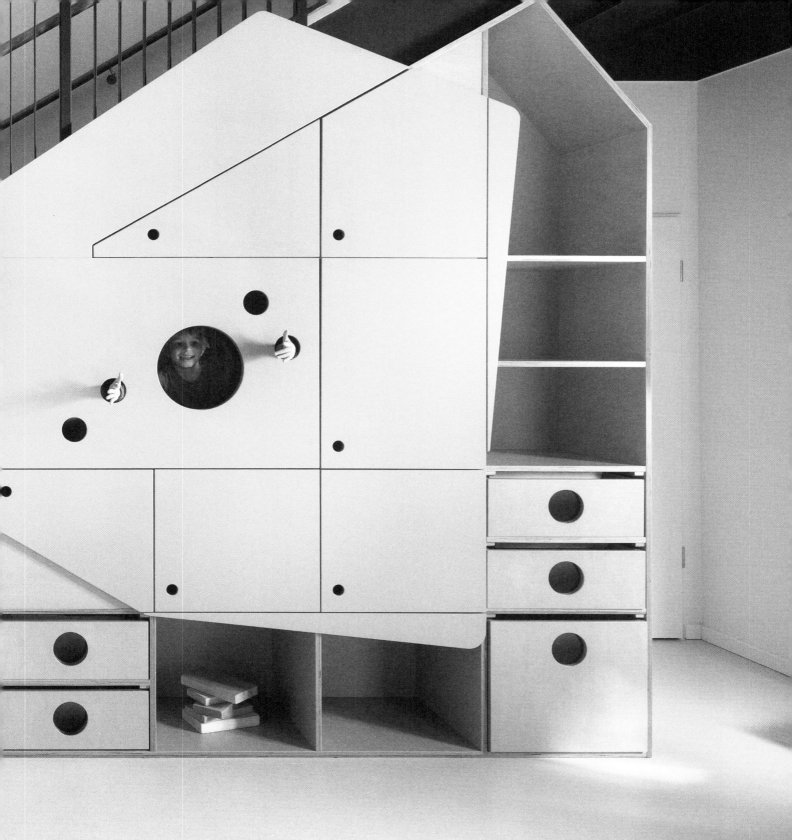

Shelves and cupboards under the stairs offer storage space for sports equipment while doubling as a three-dimensional cave and climbing world

The ground floor houses the centerpiece of the daycare center: the children's restaurant. The kitchen opens up towards the dining room, so that the children know where and how the food is prepared and can participate in the kitchen work. Outside of mealtimes, it is used as a sports and exercise room.

A slide runs parallel to the stairs. The space under and next to the stairs has been converted into a climbing frame. Floe-like protrusions allow children to climb and hide or can be used to stow away mats and sports equipment.

The solid wood furniture is modular and designed for space-saving stowage. This allows the children's restaurant to be quickly converted into an open area.

The staircase as an extra space for movement, with a slide and climbing frame

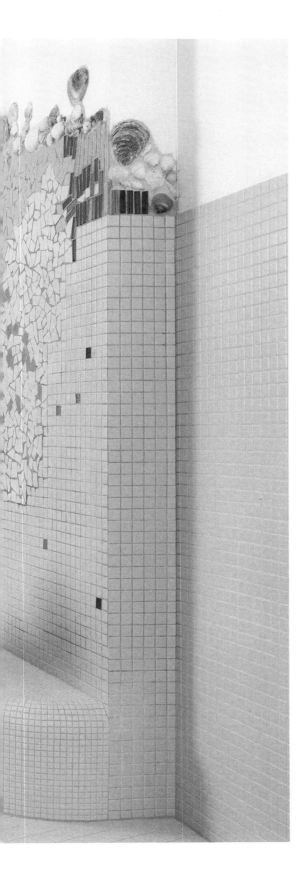

A special highlight at the CompanyKids Daycare Center is the water world on the upper floor: a bathing landscape with several basins and a big splashing area for hours of playing with water.

The wall above the splashing pool was designed in a joint workshop with the staff and mosaic artist Jana Wolf. Finds such as shells, pebbles and tile fragments were put together as a mosaic. The organic design vocabulary gives the pool a vibrant character.

Stepped stone basins, accessible from three sides, encourage playing together with water. The children not only experience the element of water with all its facets but at the same time train their communication skills. They must negotiate, assert themselves and exchange ideas, because there are only a limited number of taps.

The fitting of acoustic ceilings and underfloor heating, as well as the use of natural materials such as wood, create a warm and inviting atmosphere. This children's bathroom is a space that is used for full educational purposes.

Natural stone pools
with cascades encourage
communal water play

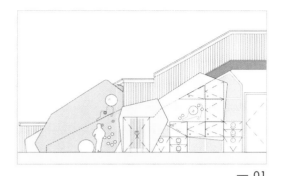

— 01

— 02

— 03

From first sketches to the daycare center

— 01

— 02

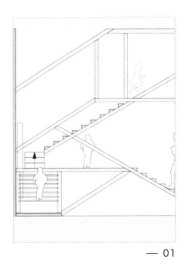

— 01

— 02

— 03

14

Flash your teeth at fear

Children's Dental Practice Kinderlieb
260 m²
Hamburg / 2018

**A relaxed atmosphere in the waiting room
— the Children's Dental Practice Kinderlieb
in Hamburg becomes a place of wellbeing.**

Pedagogy/philosophy — At the Children's Dental Practice Kinderlieb, design is not just about children's teeth but about supporting children through their treatment so that they feel confident and are not afraid. A relaxed atmosphere in the waiting room helps to overcome fear. Various games keep children occupied, distract them and reduce tension before their treatments.

Architecture — A colorful world was created across 260 square meters, which questions the conventional image of a medical practice. At the same time, all the rooms are arranged in the layout so that work processes can be optimized. All the areas, including the corridors, were incorporated into the design. The procedures at a medical practice must run as smoothly as possible: every minute is planned and counts. Both the complex technical aspects and the needs of children had to be taken into account from the first planning of the layout.

Concept — The main idea for the concept was the question of how design can help reduce fear and how to make children feel more confident. A balance between room for movement and retreat, complemented by sound and light effects, offers children a range of options for

overcoming their fear. Play platforms serve as
a stage and reading corner, a tower as a temporary
retreat with an integrated sound cave. Peepholes
at different heights allow children to watch what
is going on at the practice from a hiding place.
The natural materials and the subtle basic colors

are complemented by more vibrant shades.
Each of the four treatment rooms is designed
in one of the accent colors, and even the
corridors are incorporated into the overall
concept in terms of color, guiding patients
through the practice.

The reception counter is designed at children's height, with space for baby strollers.

In the waiting room there is a climbing tower with a cave, a reading platform and a natural wood tree.

Each treatment room is decorated in one of the accent colors.

For the Children's Dental Practice Kinderlieb in Hamburg, the child-appropriate design of their interiors is just as important as age-appropriate dental treatment. On the one hand, the personnel interact with the children kindly, and on the other hand, the design of the interior space ensures an anxiety-free atmosphere.

Every child is different and develops their own strategies for dealing with emotions in unusual situations. In order to ease tension, the play tower and the natural wood tree in the waiting room encourage activity. For children, the climbing trees are a welcome challenge, and at the same time children see from the adults' perspective from the top branches. The cave in the centrally positioned tower is a safe hide-out and a place to relax.

Sound and lighting effects in the tower hide-out entice the children into other worlds. The more relaxed the children are, the less scary the treatment will seem. The effect of architecture is used to create an environment that can counteract fear and ease tension.

Acoustic ceilings ensure pleasant room acoustics, support speech intelligibility and ease outer and inner unrest. Communication and interaction take place on a big orange pinboard. While this board serves the parents as an information portal, the children bring it to life with their drawings. All these features allow the design of interior spaces at the Kinderlieb dental practice to turn the otherwise very unpopular waiting time before the treatment into a positive experience.

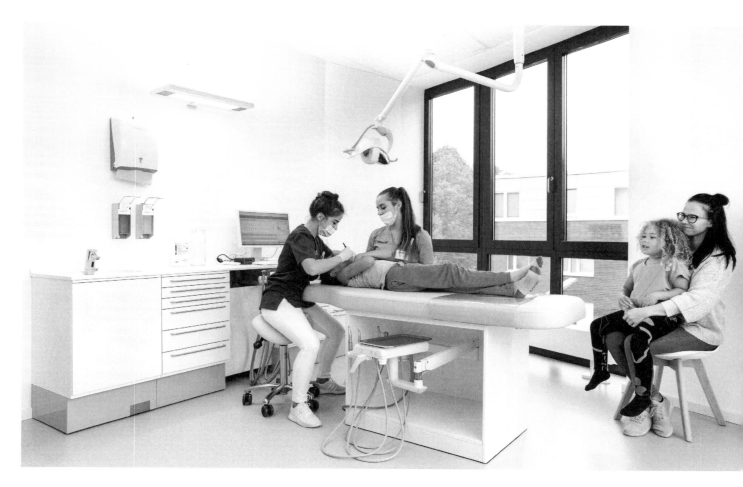

Each treatment room also has a seat for parents and siblings

The reception desk is adapted to the scale of the children, signalling: this place is for you!

Already in the entrance area it's clear who this space is designed for. As the reception counter slopes down to one side, the children can meet the reception staff at their own eye level. Eliminating such visual barriers that children face all the time in everyday life sends a first welcoming signal. This message is continued in the waiting and treatment rooms and all the way down to the children's bathroom.

With its empathetic approach, the Kinderlieb Children's Dental Practice has succeeded in creating a synthesis of DIN standards and a feel-good atmosphere radiating friendliness, which appeals to parents, the whole team and especially the very young patients.

After their successful treatment, the children can reach into the tree stump and fish out a little toy – a parting reward, relating to a child-appropriate story. The idea of the gift from the tree stump refers to Pippi Longstocking: her magical tree always has a bottle of fresh lemonade ready for her.

After the treatment, there's a reward waiting for the children in the tree stump

Seating niches in the corridors serve as additional waiting areas where children can be on their own

While dental practices for adults are usually pure white or neutral, a children's dental practice can be more colorful, because light and colors have positive effects on children's mood. The color concept was created in close cooperation with the dentist.

The colors range in the spectrum of pink, orange, red and violet, dominating not only the waiting room but also all of the five treatment rooms. From the wall design to the furnishings and work clothing of the staff, the interior of the children's dental practice is based on this warm and striking world of color. Blue shades, by contrast, are to be found only in the bathroom. Thanks to a small children's bathroom, children can go to the toilet independently without their parents. Independence increases self-confidence – a good tool against fear.

"For boys, the pink room is never an issue, only for some parents."

— **Dr. Susann Özel / children's dentist**

Every treatment room is immersed in warm light with the help of indirect lighting. The furnishings were developed in close cooperation with a dental practice fitter. The special children's reclining seats are color-coordinated to match the respective accent color of the treatment rooms.

The considerate design in combination with this striking color canon helps the children flash their teeth at fear.

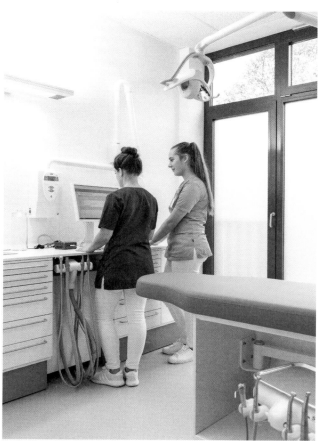

The color concept combines the architecture, furnishings and work clothing of the staff

— 01

— 02

From first sketches to the practice

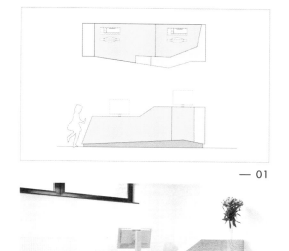

— 01

— 02

— 03

— 01

— 02

— 03

— 04

15

Colorful niches to experience

KiKu Kinderland Daycare Center
1010m² for 100 children
Berlin / 2019

The light and inviting KiKu Kinderland Daycare Center with a large outdoor area offers ample open space with hidden worlds of experience.

Pedagogy — Esteem, respect and the conviction that children are of equal value, that they are self-responsible and participating human beings, characterize the educational stance of the KiKu Kinderland Daycare Denter. Apart from this basic conviction, one of the most important aims of the provider Kinderzentren Kunterbunt GmbH is to achieve a balance between work and family life. The educational concept is based on the four pillars of co-construction, participation, inclusion and an educational partnership with the families. Apart from childcare, the families are supported by a range of additional services, and the premises are used even after daycare hours. This forges social contacts.

Architecture — In Berlin-Mahlsdorf, a two-story new building with a large outdoor area for 100 children was developed. In terms of construction, the extremely long and narrow site had to be taken into consideration, resulting in an elongated building that is structured by alternating recesses and protrusions.

The recesses in the building form niches and bays that can be animated, whether they are an urban garden, a sound installation, mirror cubicle or stage – these experience niches can be explored with the senses; they can be seen and heard.

Concept — Apart from designing a stimulating world of experience for children, the wish to open the daycare center towards the surroundings and the neighborhood was incorporated into the concept. The daycare center was not supposed to represent a foreign body in the residential area but be a vibrant addition to the quarter. To achieve this, the daycare center's forecourt has an open design and the site fence is set back. This creates a meeting place for the neighborhood – a place where the quarter and the generations can come together, talk and experience a sense of community.

"A facade must be more than protective and beautiful. It should inspire play."

— Nathalie Dziobek-Bepler / baukind

The whole building was completed in just nine months using modular construction. The niches and protrusions break up the long building volume and unify the design. The recesses in the building are clad with larch glazed in color.

Powder-coated sheet metal elements in the color of the brush stroke plaster and the almost seamless transition from wood cladding to plaster show the architects' attention to detail.

The niches structure the building; they offer a range of surprises and possibilities for the children to explore, observe and experience. The building becomes a place for an exploratory journey.

The facade is not only a protective shell but also appeals to children's imagination. Children can individually pursue their needs for retreat, shared activity or quiet play and look for their own personal niche – a stage niche for exciting experiences, a plant niche for urban gardening, a sound niche, a mirror niche and a niche with a barefoot path. The colors of the niches in the outer facade – shades of orange, yellow and red – correspond to the colors of the client's corporate design.

The stage niche with a
seating gallery becomes
an open-air theater

The multipurpose room can be used as a community room for neighborhood meetings and family activities.

Stage niche with seating gallery.

Multifunctional pedestals in the outdoor space — for playing and spending time.

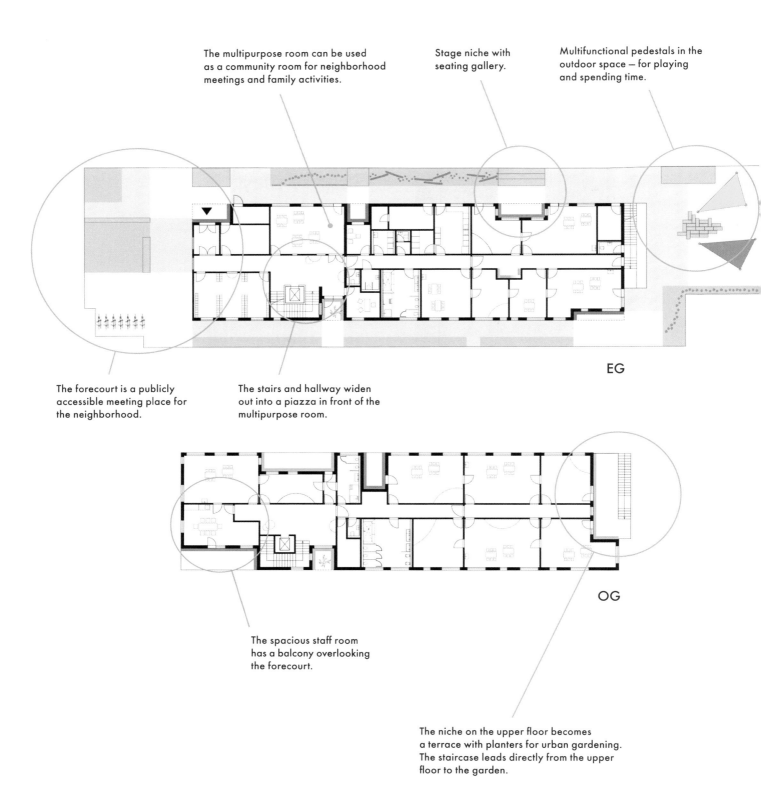

EG

The forecourt is a publicly accessible meeting place for the neighborhood.

The stairs and hallway widen out into a piazza in front of the multipurpose room.

OG

The spacious staff room has a balcony overlooking the forecourt.

The niche on the upper floor becomes a terrace with planters for urban gardening. The staircase leads directly from the upper floor to the garden.

Large open spaces with
play and climbing units,
sandboxes, seating areas,
lawns and paved paths.

Playschools are usually separated by a fence from neighboring sites and the road. Parents and children enter the site through a gate. However, this is different at the KiKu Kinderland Daycare Center: an open forecourt invites the neighborhood to share use of the space, to communicate and experience a sense of community.

The forecourt as a social venue corresponds to the philosophy of the client, who wants to allow children to experience an open society. The daycare center should not be an isolated institution but part of community life, spanning different generations. In the entrance area of the 1000-square-meter, two-story building, there is a cloakroom for 100 children.

The adjoining, open stairwell is designed as a piazza on the ground floor. Here, children,

teaching staff and parents can meet to chat and play. A large multipurpose room is also located in the entrance zone. It is used as a children's restaurant, as a sports room and for daycare parties.

The younger children are taken care of on the ground floor. Each group has a group room with direct access to the garden and an adjoining group room that serves as a sleep or relaxation room.

The older children are taken care of on the upper floor. The rooms are organized as themed rooms that enable open work. A research room, a room for role play and a craft room offer a variety of activities. The terrace on the upper floor provides direct access to the garden for the older children too.

The wall to the neighboring site is divided into sections with blackboard paint, becoming a play object. Large-format wall areas for creative painting are thus created.

The blackboard areas on the openly designed forecourt can be painted on by both the daycare children and people from the neighborhood. This opens up a communication window to the surrounding district.

Invitations and announcements for events, colorful greetings from children to their parents, or the chalk graffiti of a teenager from the neighborhood all have their place here.

The entrance area invites people from the neighborhood to spend time, while offering space for shared activities

Windows at children's height — adjusting the
scale to children is the focus of the design

The recesses in the facade form niches in the interior. A niche completely clad with mirrors blurs one's spatial perception and carries the viewer off into unknown dimensions.

In the interiors of the KiKu Kinderland Daycare Center, the circle was chosen as a guiding design element. There are big circles on the walls, round hatches and interior windows.

Each group is assigned its own color scheme, which makes orientation easier for the children in the 1000-square-meter building.

The play of windows at different heights, adapted to the height of children, draws attention to the perspective of the little ones. In line with pedagogue Maria Montessori: "It is not the child who should adapt to the environment, but we who should adapt the environment to the child." The change in scale accords the children respect and recognition.

The mirror niche dissolves familiar perceptions of space and of oneself

Round hatches create spatial connections that only children can fit through

"In our facilities, we focus on one thing in particular: the true compatibility of family and work."

— Björn Czinczoll / Kunterbunt Children's Centers

A seating and climbing landscape
for children and adults

Behind the building, the site opens towards a large garden with play elements and areas of greenery. The cubic design concept is continued here and reflected in the platforms and multifunctional climbing and seating landscape. This provides climbing and movement incentives for children and simultaneously serves as a meeting place and seating for adults.

The paved paths can be used by all kinds of children's vehicles and also serve as a surface for large-scale chalk drawings.

Large areas of sand structure the outdoor space and offer good fall protection beneath the climbing equipment. Awnings, hammocks and decorations can be affixed to the robinia trunks. The outdoor area thus becomes a place for festive gatherings – in everyday daycare life or with the family and neighbors.

— 01

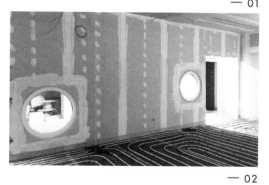

— 02

— 03

From first sketches to the daycare center

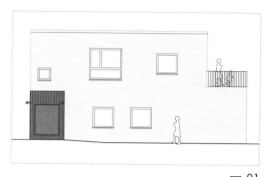

— 01

— 02

— 03

— 01

— 02

Thanks

— for this book

Publisher and editing — jovis Verlag, Doris Kleilein, Nina Kathalin Bergeest, Tim Vogel, Katharina Freisinger / Translator — Lynne Kolar-Thompson, Michael Thomas Taylor / Concept — Nathalie Dziobek-Bepler, Rea Naber, Lena Arnold / Text — Jeanette Kunsmann (pp. 10–19, 80–91, 146–157), Stephan Weiner, Nora Heinz, Nathalie Dziobek-Bepler, Lena Arnold, Miriam Lösch / Graphic design — Rea Naber / Interviews — Karin Schmidt-Ruhland, Markus Schindler

— to you, amazing baukind team

Alina Lorenz / Anna-Lea Wiegard / Benita Wetzel / Carla Herrero / Chaisi Glover / Christian Edlinger / Christian Stockschlaeder / Claudia Reimann / Dorothee Brosche / Gil Ja Geiss / Heike Heister / Ivonne Schäfer / Johanne Schlottmann / Josefine Peters / Kathia Ecks / Katja Höpfner / Kristina Leikauf / Lena Arnold / Lidya Yengül / Luka-Sophie Herr / Magdalena Böttcher / Majd Abboud / Mareike Hupfer / Maria Opel / Mathilde Gaudin / Milena Monssen / Miriam Lösch / Nadine Kölble / Nadine Schimmelpfennig / Naja Spohner / Nathalie Dziobek-Bepler / Nicole Schneider / Paulina Grebenstein / Petra Holthöfer / Pia Uibeleisen / Rea Naber / Sascha Arndt / Serena Cerillo / Svetlana Ralew

— for the valuable years together

Lilia Kleemann from papoq greatly contributed to the development of baukind as a founder for many years. Without you, baukind would not be what it is today!

— to our dear clients

For trusting, inspiring and challenging us!

— for the beautiful images

Anne Deppe / Boris Breuer / Christoph Musiol / Corinna und Philipp Langenheim von HEJM / Marcus Ebener / Julia Geiss / Udo Meinel / Werner Hutmacher / Julia Hafenscher / Robert Sanow / Petra Stockhausen / Matthias Ritzmann / Matthias Lüdecke

— to our super supermodels

Aaron / Anuk / Anuri / Ava / Bara / Bobby / Cameron / Christian / Clara / Edith / Edward / Elian / Enno / Fanny / Gwendolyn / Hannah Katharina / Harald / Holly / Janosch / Jimmy / Johanna / Jolie / Jonas / Josefine / Josepha / Juna / Karl / Kiki / Laura / Lennard / Léonie / Liou / Lothar / Luke / Maia / Mara / Mathilde / Milo / Minou / Neva / Nike / Paloma / Reza / Robin / Sabrina / Stefanie / Susann / Tallulah / Tom / Wilma / Yong Tak / alle baukinder

— for your trust, love and support

Alexander Schwedeler / Anne Freiberger-Liebscher / Arne Keunecke / Badabaum / Badaboom / Bernadette Saul / Bianca & Sven Arnold / Brigitte & Frank Dziobek / Claus Meusel / Daniela Andresen / Daniel Richter / Elisabeth Gravier / Gabriele Batliner / Henning Grupe / In Ja Geiss / Iris Bonowsky / Prof. Dr. Isabel Dziobek / Joann Bäker-Ibrahim / Jonathan Bepler / Jörg DeBreuyn / Dr. Jürgen Reul / Katrin Schleicher / Kerstin Hippler / Klaus McKenzie / LA21 / Leo Lipp / Marc Nutsch / Margit Werner / Martin Hübner / Michael Fischer / Michael Pfau / Modul / Monika & Robert Schieferdecker / Mirjam Spitalsky / Nadine Dziobek / Peggy Laubinger / Peter Deluse / Philipp Ikels / Sanne Ertbirk / Sinikka Kühn / Stefanie Vieira-Mykoniatis / Dr. Susann Özel / U-Institut / Ulrich Böttger / Ulrich Klier / Dr. Ute Gerwert / Vera Kögler

— Bibliography

1 — Hebenstreit, Sigurd: Maria Montessori, Herder, Freiburg im Breisgau 1999, p. 61

2 — Walden, Rotraut (ed.), Kosica, Simone (author): Architekturpsychologie für Kindertagesstätten, Pabst Science Publishers, Lengenrich 2011, p. 5

3 — Aden-Grossmann, Wilma: Der Kindergarten – Geschichte, Entwicklung, Konzepte, Beltz, Weinheim 2011, pp. 32–33

4 — Juul, Jesper: Dein kompetentes Kind, Rowohlt Taschenbuch Verlag, Hamburg 2016, p. 24

5 — Fröbel, Friedrich: Der Menschenerziehung, Verlag der Allgemeinen Deutschen Erziehungsanstalt, Keilhau 1826, p. 26

6 — Fröbel, Friedrich: Der Menschenerziehung, Verlag der Allgemeinen Deutschen Erziehungsanstalt, Keilhau 1826, p. 16

7 — Waldschmidt, Ingeborg: Maria Montessori – Leben und Werk, C.H.Beck, Munich 2010, p. 41

8 — Hoffmann, Johanna: Spiele fürs Leben, Greifenverlag, Rudolstadt 1971, p. 162

9 — Breithecker, Dieter: Bewegung braucht das Kind ... damit es sich gesund entwickeln und wohlfühlen kann, Wehrfritz Wissenschaftlicher Dienst, 2002, no. 76, p. 3

10 — Dirx, Ruth: Das Kind, das unbekannte Wesen – Geschichte, Soziologie, Pädagogik, von Schröder, Hamburg 1964, p. 147

— Images

Julia Hafenscher — pp. 1, 2

Christoph Musiol — p. 7

HEJM — pp. 9, 11, 14, 16, 17, 21, 22 left + middle, 23 left + middle, 24 right, 27, 29 bottom, 30 left + right, 31, 31 bottom, 33, 34 top, 39 left + right, 45 left, 46, 54, 55 bottom, 57 middle bottom + bottom, 58 oben + left, 60, 69 left, 70 top, 71, 72, 73 top, 76 left, 77, 87 bottom right, 91 left, 92–127, 146–173

Anne Deppe — pp. 12, 22 right, 23 right, 24 left + bottom, 26, 28, 29 top, 32 top + middle, 34 left + right, 35, 28 middle + right, 39 middle, 41 bottom, 42 top, 43, 44 top, 45 top + middle + bottom, 47, 48, 49, 51, 52 middle + right, 53, 56, 57 top + middle top, 58 right, 59, 61, 62, 63 left + right, 64, 65, 67, 68, 69 right, 70 left, 73 left + right, 74, 75 left top + middle left + middle right + bottom, 76 right, 78, 79, 86, 87 top left + top right + bottom left, 128–145

Udo Meinel — pp. 15, 37, 38 left, 40, 41 top + right

Marcus Ebener — pp. 30 bottom, 42 bottom, 55 top, 63 bottom, 70 right, 75 top right

Werner Hutmacher — pp. 44 bottom, 52 left

Mattias Ritzmann — p. 81 left

Petra Stockhausen — p. 81 right

Mattias Lüdecke — p. 91 right

Impressum

Cover image — Anne Deppe, daycare center Unterm Regenschirm in Berlin

Photographs — Anne Deppe / Boris Breuer / Christoph Musiol / Corinna and Philipp Langenheim – HEJM / Marcus Ebener / Julia Geiss / Udo Meinel / Werner Hutmacher / Julia Hafenscher / Robert Sanow / Petra Stockhausen / Matthias Ritzmann / Matthias Lüdecke

Project management — Tim Vogel
Editing — Katharina Freisinger, Michael Thomas Taylor
Translator — Lynne Kolar-Thompson, Michael Thomas Taylor
Design and typesetting — Rea Naber
Lithography — Rea Naber
Printed in the European Union

Bibliographic information of the German National Library
The German National Library has recorded this publication in the German national bibliography; detailed bibliographic information is available on the Internet at http://dnb.d-nb.de.

jovis Verlag GmbH
Lützowstraße 33
10785 Berlin

www.jovis.de

jovis books are available worldwide in the selected book trade. Information about our international distribution is available from your book retailer or at www.jovis.de

ISBN 978-3-86859-717-2